MODELLING
HAPPINESS

A Guide for Teachers & Parents

REEN ROSE

ISBN-13: 978-0-9939883-2-5

ISBN-10: 0993988326

For Emily and Drew

Contents

Section III – The Precepts

Foreword

This is a book about change, choice, and happiness.

Statistics show that young people in our society are struggling to create lives of robust happiness. This is my term for happiness that is resilient and long-lasting. Being robustly happy rarely happens by chance.

Happiness is a choice. Only you can make that choice, but you need skills, strategies, and understanding before that can happen. When children are very young, they rely on the guidance of their parents and other significant adults in their lives for a feeling of well-being. As they grow, they need to learn how to create robustly happy lives for themselves. To help them with this endeavor, it's important to provide them with tools, knowledge, and strategies.

Children model themselves after the important adults in their lives. The most vital thing you can do if you want your students and children to be happy, is to model the behaviors you want them to adopt.

The Modelling Happiness program includes eight precepts that are based on scientific research. A precept is a principle for action. Each one is designed to increase your understanding of the supporting science, and is accompanied by strategies to help put it into action.

I've written this book primarily for teachers and parents, so they can help the children under their care to lead robustly happy lives, but the precepts work just as well for people and organizations from all walks of life. If you are the manager of a company, modelling happiness and sharing these precepts can have just as significant an effect on your team or employees as it can for teachers and their students.

By learning what science knows about positive emotions and becoming a happiness model, you can help change the world, one child, one class, one school at a time.

Acknowledgements

They say that everyone has at least one book in them, and I am sure that is true, although to get a book into the world you need to have a great team to support you. I would like to acknowledge a few members of my book writing circle.

My first thank you is to Alionka Polanco. It was during a half-day coaching session together that she suggested I write this book. I needed her spark to fire me into action.

Thank you to my editor Emily Swan, and to my psychology consultant, Gordon Rose. They are the ones who ensure that my thoughts make sense to more than just me. The more eyes you get on a manuscript the better, and these two sets of eyes are invaluable.

I would like to acknowledge Sandy Magee of Red Sand Creative, who designed the beautiful cover. He is incredibly easy to work with, and his creativity and skills are amazing.

Thank you to everyone who supported me in my project. You are too numerous to include by name, but know that your words of encouragement, and support were instrumental in this book's inception and completion. I am blessed to have so many wonderful people in my life.

Finally, I would like to thank my husband, children, and parents for keeping me company on my journey. You have been with me through the good times and the bad, and have loved me every step of the way.

Section I –
Building a Foundation

Happiness & Positive Psychology

Happiness is a word that means different things to each of us, so let me start by establishing what I mean when I talk about happiness.

Happiness is the umbrella that covers every positive feeling or emotion. If you prefer, substitute a word like satisfaction, joy, contentment, or any other feel-good word that holds a stronger meaning for you. The last thing I want is for anyone to get bogged down in semantics. This book is about learning skills to live a life that contains more feelings of overall positivity than negativity - whatever that means to you.

When the study of positive psychology was in its infancy, scientists struggled with how to measure feelings. How do you know if someone is happy or not? How do you conduct research when you can't standardize the meaning of happiness and there is no concrete way to measure it?

Ed Diener solved this predicament when he came up with the term 'subjective well-being.' This expression suggests that people should self-evaluate to determine their level of happiness, rather than leaving it to be established by scientists.

Following this way of thinking, it doesn't matter what type of emotion you are experiencing or if other people agree with you. If you think you are feeling content, then you are in a state of positive well-being; if *you* believe you are stressed, then you are in a state of negative well-being. We'll explore this idea further in the section on Perception.

Historically, psychology was devoted to the study of

mental illness. Research was largely aimed at finding ways to help mentally afflicted individuals live more satisfying lives. The introduction of positive psychology meant a break with tradition; armed with both a definition and a strategy to measure emotion, positive psychology was ready to discover more about the behavior and the minds of mentally healthy individuals.

The breakthrough for this discipline happened in 1998, when Martin Seligman became president of the American Psychology Association. As an advocate for this brand of psychology, he decided that the time had come to study mentally healthy people and discover new ways to help them live happier lives.

Since its pronouncement, positive psychology research has exploded with studies and discoveries. These scientific findings are the basis for the precepts and strategies included in this book; I'll be sharing the findings of relevant research studies throughout.

Why Happiness is Important

Thousands of studies have been carried out since Martin Seligman encouraged the scientific world to embrace positive psychology as a legitimate branch of science. Psychologists have discovered that people who experience a consistent feeling of well-being in their lives have many advantages over unhappy people.

Aside from the obvious advantage of feeling good about yourself and your life, research shows happy people:

- Are more successful
- Have more friends, stronger support networks, and better social lives
- Are more likely to have healthy minds and bodies
- Live longer
- Are more successful in job interviews
- Have stronger immune systems
- Are more productive
- Have better home lives
- Are promoted faster
- Are more motivated and engaged
- Are more creative
- Are more resilient to change and challenge
- Experience less stress

This is not a comprehensive list, but hopefully you can see

just how important it is to create classrooms and homes that encourage happiness. If we want to foster students and children who are good leaders, successful, motivated and engaged, we need to ensure they have the skills, knowledge, and precepts necessary to create happy lives for themselves.

Our Emotional State Today

Just because someone has a smile on their face, it doesn't mean they are happy. Think of Robin Williams, the brilliant comedian and actor who was always smiling and using his gift of humor to make people laugh. The world was shocked when the news was released that he had committed suicide.

People who struggle on the inside frequently don't show it on the outside. The statistics show that there are many young people who are struggling to create a life that seems worth living, and often they never discuss what they are going through with anybody. They try to find an answer all by themselves.

It may be strange to say that they are on the right track, but in a strange way, they are. I'm not suggesting that you should struggle by yourself, without getting any assistance, but it is important for you to understand that you are responsible for your own happiness. Entrusting your positive well-being to other people puts you in an extremely precarious position. What if that person disappears out of your life? Do you know how to make yourself happy without them?

The problem so often encountered by young people looking for an answer to the question of happiness is that they don't know where to look. They haven't been equipped with happiness skills they can put into action. The only strategy left at their disposal is confiding in someone else, and if they don't feel comfortable doing that, they are left floundering.

The number of people of all ages who suffer from

depression is staggering. Although many depressed people never consider suicide, adolescents with depressive illnesses have a higher rate of suicidal thinking and behavior.

According to the Canadian Mental Health Association website, almost one in four deaths among fifteen to twenty-four year-olds is from suicide. For Canadian adults aged twenty-five to forty-four, 16% of all deaths are due to suicide. Those are statistics we can't afford to ignore.

Let me share a few more facts from this same source:

- Suicide is among the leading causes of death for fifteen to twenty-four year-old Canadians, second only to accidents; 4,000 people die prematurely each year by suicide
- A staggering 3.2 million Canadians, aged twelve to nineteen, are currently at risk for developing depression
- It is estimated that 10-20% of Canadian youths are affected by a mental illness or disorder – the single most disabling group of disorders worldwide
- Suicide is one of the leading causes of death for both men and women from adolescence to middle age
- The suicide mortality rate among men is four times the rate among women
- Today, approximately 5% of male youths and 12% of female youths, aged twelve to nineteen, have experienced a major depressive episode
- Surpassed only by injuries, mental disorders in youths are ranked as the second highest hospital care expenditure in Canada
- In Canada, only 20% of children who need mental health services receive them
- Approximately 8% of adults will experience major depression at some time in their lives

- 20% of all Canadians will personally experience a mental illness in their lifetime
- Almost one half (49%) of those who feel they have suffered from depression or anxiety have never gone to see a doctor about this problem

Things aren't any better in the United States or Britain.

According to the UK charity Young Minds:

- One in four (26%) young people in the UK experience suicidal thoughts
- Among teenagers, rates of depression and anxiety have increased by 70% in the past twenty-five years, particularly since the mid 1980's
- 55% of children who have been bullied develop depression as adults

The Jason Foundation website has these figures listed for youth suicide statistics in the United States:

- Suicide is the second leading cause of death for young people aged ten to twenty-four
- More teenagers and young adults die from suicide than from cancer, heart disease, AIDS, birth defects, stroke, pneumonia, influenza, and chronic lung disease *combined*
- Each day in the USA, there are an average of over 5,240 suicide attempts by young people in grades 7-12
- Four out of five teens who attempt suicide have displayed clear warning signs

It is impossible not to feel concerned for youths world-wide, when so many are suffering from unhappiness, anxiety, and depression. Few people have ever been taught happiness skills, so if you aren't one of the lucky ones, it's hard to know what to do when you need a boost of positivity. Add the stigma that mental illness still holds and it's easy to see how we are falling short when it comes to helping our children, teenagers, and young adults.

My Happiness Story

I have a very personal reason for writing this book, as well as for working with schools and parent associations to improve the level of mental well-being our young people possess. Some people may be interested in the events that led me to where I am today. If you aren't one of those people, please skip over this section; I promise not to hold it against you, or give away any vital information that you will wish you hadn't missed.

I was a very happy person for the first thirty years of my life. That doesn't mean that my life was perfect - far from it. I had ups and downs and bad hair days, but I was confident that everything in my life would work out for the best in the end. It always had so far. This belief allowed me to move to new places and try new things with a certain level of confidence.

Incidentally, I still believe that whatever happens in my life will turn out to be a good thing, even if I can't make sense of it right away. I will talk more about this principle in the precepts that follow.

When I had been teaching in British Columbia for six years, I applied to the commonwealth teaching exchange program. If the organization can find a teacher in another commonwealth country that is a good fit for the classes you teach, they arrange for you to swap homes and jobs for a year.

I was matched with a teacher from my chosen exchange country of England, and so I set off on a twelve-month adventure. I was confident that I would have an amazing time and come home better than ever.

Toward the end of my year in the UK, I met an English man and fell madly in love. The good news? I was in love. The bad news? My twelve-month exchange was almost over; I was due to be back in Canada in a few months to continue my teaching contract.

It may have been a moment of madness, but we decided that our best course of action was to make our relationship more permanent. Ten weeks after we met, we were engaged, and before the year was over, we were married.

We decided to set up home in England. I had already spent a year living there and loved it, so it seemed to make sense. I wouldn't be in the same part of the country, but how different could the midlands be to London?

As always, I felt confident in my decision. Everything had always worked out for me in the past, so why should this be any different? I headed into the new adventure with the belief I would shortly be living my happily ever after.

Things started out well, but slowly I found my new life was starting to take its toll. Living in a small village in the centre of England was vastly different to living in a bustling, vibrant place like London. I was trying to get my teaching credentials accepted, but in the interim I took a full-time position in a clothing store. It was just a job to keep me going until I could teach.

I can't explain how much I missed my teaching career. My husband had started a new job and had an exciting life of connections and social events. I joined him for many of these things, but they weren't my friends or colleagues, and I felt completely out of place.

Staying in touch with my family and friends was difficult. The internet was in its infancy and phone calls were expensive.

It didn't happen overnight, but as those first few years

passed, I fell into a deep pit of despair. Mood disorders are common in my family. I believed I had escaped the family curse, but that wasn't the case. After a couple of years in my new life, I barely recognized the face that stared back at me in the mirror. I had no idea what was happening to me, but I wasn't happy and life seemed to get bleaker by the day.

As I mentioned earlier, it isn't always easy to see that someone is struggling mentally. If you knew me then, or even if you know me now, you might find it hard to believe that I suffer from depression. I learned from an early age that my best way of surviving was to smile and laugh. I became a great actress. I could always put a smile on my face, even though I was dying inside.

I went through a few months of being sick with one illness or another - constantly. After visiting my doctor for the fifth time in a couple of months, he picked up on the real cause of my sicknesses.

When I told my husband and in-laws that the doctor thought I was depressed and had prescribed me anti-depressants, they urged me to keep that information to myself and come off the medication as soon as possible. They were worried about the side effects of the drug and that people would think I was crazy if they found out I was depressed. Mental illness was, and still is, widely misunderstood. Their intentions came from the heart, but only served to make me feel ashamed of what I was going through. I only took the medication for a month and kept my struggles to myself; I wasn't strong enough to question whether this decision was right for me or not.

I was in a very dark place, convinced that life wasn't worth living and that no one would even notice if I was gone. I spent my time thinking about the best way to end it all. This is the dire place I was in when I discovered the shocking and totally unexpected news that I was pregnant.

I like to think of it as divine intervention, because learning I was pregnant was a game changer. I knew that, for the sake of my unborn child, I had to find a way out of that pit – and I did, although I still wasn't dancing my happy dance.

Awareness is the first step to transformation; I had no idea how I was going to go from battered to balanced, but I was determined to find a way. I wasn't sure what had made me happy to start with, so it was difficult to know how to recapture it.

When I look back on those happy early decades of my life, I realize that my family and friends had taken responsibility for my happiness, and without even realizing it, I had let them. When I got married and moved away, they were no longer in a position to do that, and without saying anything, they trusted that my husband would pick up the ball.

My lovely husband was not raised to be ruled by duty the way my family was, and without consciously deciding to decline the task of making me happy, that's what he did.

Meanwhile, I was modelling the example my parents had set for me: I looked to my husband to make me happy. I was frustrated that he didn't seem able to sprinkle happy dust on me and transform my life, and that put a huge strain on our relationship. I think it's fair to say that during much of the next two decades of my life, I struggled to find a way out of my emotional predicament.

I wasn't just searching to find a happier place for myself, I wanted to ensure my children didn't find themselves in a similar situation.

I realize now that although I was a very loved and cared-for child, I wasn't equipped with the information and skills necessary to be robustly happy. I didn't have the right emotional state to withstand challenges and tough times. My happiness had been fragile, and shattered when my circumstances changed.

The person who seemed to be the cause of my unhappiness was ultimately the one who helped me turn my life around. Without my husband forcing me to take responsibility for my own mental well-being, I may well have been emotionally dependent on other people for my entire life.

I began researching what science had uncovered about happiness and discovered that the only person who could make me happy was me. This realization gave me power over my own destiny, and made me stronger. The strategy my mother had modelled for me had put me in a very vulnerable position, and I was determined to model a better strategy for my children.

As I learned more about positivity, I implemented those strategies into my parenting and shared what I knew with my children. I resolved to do everything I could to put them into a stronger position to live happy lives than I had been.

I have watched my daughter and son grow into adults who understand the importance of taking responsibility for their own happiness. This doesn't mean I'm suggesting you should only be looking out for number one, to the detriment of everyone else around you. I encourage you to become proactive, making choices and taking responsibility, rather than crossing your fingers and hoping fate deals you a good hand.

The statistics show how common it is to feel hopeless and helpless. This proves just how important it is to teach happiness skills to young people, providing them with the necessary attitudes and understandings to be robustly happy.

Section II -
The Science Behind the Precepts

Brain Basics

I believe it is important to understand a little bit about how the brain works if you want to capitalize on using its power. By knowing what's happening when you're learning a new skill or practicing something difficult, it can make it easier to persevere rather than give up. It also gives you more confidence to make choices that will result in a greater level of happiness.

Brain Anatomy

The brain is divided into three parts: the cerebrum, the cerebellum, and the medulla.

The cerebrum, or cerebral cortex, makes up about 85% of the brain's weight and consists of tightly packed nerve cells called neurons. Visually, it's the wrinkly outer portion that many of us imagine when we think of the brain. The cerebrum is responsible for higher-level processes like decision-making, reasoning, memory, and language.

The cerebellum is located at the back of the brain, below the cerebrum. It plays an important part in the performing of voluntary tasks, and is essential for movement and balance.

The medulla is also known as the brain stem, and is the oldest and most vital part of the brain. It looks after involuntary functions like breathing, blinking, circulating blood, and digesting food. These are all things our body does without conscious thought. The medulla is found under the cerebrum and in front of the cerebellum. It also connects the brain to the spinal cord.

Neuroscience 101

Neurons are the specialized cells that make up the nervous system. They contain a cell body, dendrites, and an axon. Dendrites receive signals from other neurons, the cell body then processes these signals, and the axon sends signals out to the dendrites of other neurons. The axon can range in length from mere millimetres, to almost a metre.

The brain, which forms part of the nervous system, contains approximately 100 billion neurons. Each one fires on average about 200 times a second, and connects to about 1000 other neurons. Neurons send messages by transmitting electrical impulses along their axons, and receive them by accepting these impulses along their dendrites. It is like a one-way road system.

A different combination of neurons is involved for each activity the brain orchestrates. Listening, reading, speaking, and thinking all use different patterns of brain activity. Our brains create unique skill patterns for each activity we undertake repeatedly.

The cell body is gray in color, which is why some people refer to the brain as gray matter, and the fictional Belgian detective Hercule Poirot refers to his brain as his little gray cells, but there is a lot of white matter in the brain as well. Almost 50% of your brain is made up of myelin, a fatty white tissue that covers the axons of some neurons.

The process of wrapping myelin around parts of the axons is known as myelination. Its purpose is to increase the strength and speed of the electrical impulses. Rather than travelling in a straight line down the axons, impulses are forced to jump the myelin to the next open spot. This process of jumping is a much faster way for impulses to travel.

Myelination happens naturally, especially during childhood, when the brain is like a sponge that soaks up every new idea and skill it comes up against. In the adult brain, myelination is slower to develop and requires more effort, but it happens all the same.

How the Brain Learns

Humans are wired to learn intuitively, by observing, experiencing, and practicing. As you repeat the things you are learning over and over, you get better and better at doing them. New skills may feel awkward and unnatural to start with, but as you practice them, they become smoother and require less effort. This action of learning creates changes in your brain.

Everything you do, think, or feel, comes from impulses that are passed from one neural cell to another. Each skill, experience, or thought you have involves a different combination of neurons firing. The more a particular pattern is repeated, the stronger the connection between the neurons gets.

When you practice a skill, or repeat an experience, the brain triggers the same pattern of neurons, strengthening the link between them. If their connection is reinforced, it becomes more likely that they will fire together in the future. As Canadian psychologist Donald Hebb put it, 'Neurons that fire together wire together.' Conversely, if your brain stops firing a specific combination of impulses because you have stopped using that skill, your brain will eventually eliminate or 'prune' the links between those neurons.

Some years ago, scientists thought our brains could only learn new things when we were young. As we reached maturity, they thought our brains were no longer capable of creating new patterns. Fortunately, recent discoveries in the field of neuroplasticity show this is not the case.

Current research shows that the brain is capable of learning throughout an entire lifespan, although you may have to work a little harder at developing new skills than you did when you were younger. The key to success is continuing to learn new things, and practicing skills you don't want to lose competency in. 'Use it or lose it' is an apt expression.

Research shows that some regions of the adult brain stay just as flexible and ready to develop as the brain of an infant. As a lifelong learner, you can continue to create or strengthen connections in your brain throughout your entire life. This plasticity means the adult brain can change its physical structure just like a child's can.

Perfection comes from Perfect Practice

Don't spend time practicing a skill incorrectly. If you want to improve your ability to play basketball, it is no use spending hours shooting baskets if you miss every single one. If you want to increase the myelin in your brain, you need to concentrate on the quality of the practice, as well as the quantity of repetitions.

Practicing a skill poorly will not aid you in doing it better. To improve your skill level, you need to practice frequently *and* evaluate the quality of your skill. If possible, get feedback to make sure you are practicing the skill correctly. Practice will only make perfect if you are practicing it the right way.

This knowledge has an implication when it comes to homework. Asking students to practice a skill at home is only useful if they have already developed a high-quality method first, or if they have someone there who can evaluate what they are doing and help them practice it properly. Ineffective practice doesn't foster learning and isn't a good use of time.

Watch this Space

The study of neuroscience is growing in leaps and bounds. Discoveries are being made continuously, so it is important to stay up to date with new research. One area that has transformed our understanding of the brain is neurogenesis. This is the term used for the growth and development of neurons.

Until recently, scientists believed that brain cells were designed to live for a life-time, and once you reached maturity, you wouldn't create new ones. In the early 1990s, scientists demonstrated adult neurogenesis in humans and other primates. This is likely to have strong implications for the future of neurobiology, and may well lead to new understanding of our brain's ability to learn.

The Importance of Emotions

It is easy to get caught up in the pursuit of happiness and think that the ideal life is one of never-ending bliss, but that isn't reality, and if it were, humans would be on a slippery slope to extinction.

In more primitive times, when humans were competing with their environment and predators to stay alive, emotions developed to help with survival. The things that humans perceive as threats today may not be the same as when they roamed the savannah dealing with sabre-tooth tigers, but your emotions are helping you just the same.

Negative Emotions

When you understand the purpose of negative feelings, it is easier to accept them. Your goal is to deal with negative emotions in a healthy way, not to eliminate them.

I was sitting in my car before my Toastmasters group was scheduled to start. Light was only just beginning to show in the sky as it was 6.30 am. I was giving a speech that day. I've always enjoyed presenting, but on this occasion my extremely busy week meant I had written my speech just a few hours before I had gone to bed. I wasn't confident that I would remember all the points I wanted to hit, so I was having one final private run-through before I left my car.

I was totally engrossed in my task when someone knocked very loudly on my window. I started, gave a little shout, and fixed a glare on the smiling face that peered in at me. Within a fraction of a second my expression changed to a smile as I recognized who it was.

I put down the window, and with one hand on my rapidly beating heart I informed my friend Ken that he had almost given me a heart attack.

The hype and news coverage about happiness may leave you with the idea that negative emotions are harmful and should be avoided. This could not be further from the truth.

Your negative emotions are important for your growth, and vital for survival. They raise your alarm system and get you ready for a fight-or-flight response. It's like having the burglar alarm go off in a bank when an intruder enters the vault. As soon as the bank staff hear the alarm, they get ready to do what is necessary to protect themselves, the customers, and the bank's resources.

The moment your brain perceives a threat, it develops a heightened awareness of what is going on around you and prepares to respond in the way most likely to result in survival. This is known as the fight-or-flight response.

Your brain will instinctively decide to either stay and fight the threat, or take flight to get away from the danger. It's rare that you actively choose which of these responses you will follow; the decision almost always is made on a subconscious level.

Several things happen when you enter this survival mode. Chemicals like adrenaline and cortisol are released into your bloodstream; your heart speeds up and pumps extra oxygen to your muscles; blood is rerouted from your digestive tract and sent to your muscles and limbs; you become intensely aware of your surroundings; your sight becomes sharper; your impulses quicken and your perception of pain diminishes. Your body is preparing to face the danger, or run away from it.

Just because you no longer live on the savannah, or find yourself threatened by sabre toothed tigers, doesn't mean this primitive survival response has disappeared. When your body and brain perceive a threat, they still default to this reaction.

In today's society, your brain is most likely to feel threatened when it finds itself in a win-lose situation. This can happen when you are having a verbal confrontation, or if you're preparing to talk to your teacher, parent, or boss and feel uneasy about the outcome.

If you perceive there is only going to be one winner emerging from the conversation, you will flip to negative emotions to prepare yourself for the battle. In primitive times, winning meant surviving.

Negative emotions also prepare you for battle in another interesting way. Research shows when you are in a negative mindset, your ability to assess your skill level is extremely accurate. In contrast, when you are feeling positive emotions, you tend to overestimate how skilful you are. When you understand that negative emotions are designed to help you survive, being accurate in the assessment of your skill-level when you are under threat makes perfect sense.

Imagine you find yourself in a fight-or-flight situation. Perhaps you are on the savanna, gathering food, when you spot a hyena the size of a bear. Are you better off knowing that you can't possibly outrun it, or telling yourself that you're the best runner in your community, so you can escape to the safely of your tribe before he catches you? Precisely! When survival is on the line, you need to know what skills are actually at your disposal, not just the skills you hope you have.

Your reaction to threat hasn't changed since primitive

times. In the modern age, losing may not always result in death, but instinctively you still feel driven to be the winner.

When Ken knocked on the window of my car and startled me, I immediately went into a fight-or-flight response. My negative emotions were attempting to help me fight my attacker. I very quickly realized that I wasn't being threatened and felt my negative mood lift, but because hormones had been released into my bloodstream, my heart was racing and my muscles were preparing to strike out or run.

I'm sure almost everyone can relate to my experience. Sometimes we can recover quickly, and other times not so much. I remember a friend jumping out at someone to scare them as a joke, only to be punched in the face. My friend accused his attacker of not having any sense of humor, but in reality, the startled young man was acting on instinct.

If you find yourself shifting into a negative mindset, chances are very good that you are consciously, or unconsciously, perceiving a win-lose situation. The negativity is there to heighten your chances of coming out on top.

The next time you experience some type of negative emotion, stop and see if you can identify the win-lose situation your brain perceives is happening. Understanding that negative emotions are part of your fight-or-flight response can make it easier to accept your feelings, and deal with them in a positive manner. You might also find it simpler to understand and empathize with others when they shift into a negative mindset.

The Fight-or-Flight Response in Today's World

Many of the risks you encounter today are not threats to your survival, but your brain still reacts to them as if they are. If you have a conversation with someone and you begin to view it as a win-lose situation, it wouldn't be appropriate to respond by punching the other person, or running away from them. Society dictates that the right way of behaving is to remain in the conversation, and react in a mature and calm manner. This can be challenging if your body is sending you hormones and increased oxygen to enable you to fight or flee.

In today's world, when fight-or-flight isn't an appropriate way to deal with a win-lose situation, a common way of behaving is to become aggressive, and overreact to what is being said.

Think about a time when you were talking to someone who suddenly became antagonistic and responded in an overly dramatic way. You might have found yourself taking a step back and wondering what in heaven's name was wrong with them.

Can you maybe recall a time when you became hostile or overly sensitive about what a person was saying to you? If you look back on the situation, you may wonder what came over you; your reaction was totally out of character. This is the modern way of dealing with the fight-or-flight response.

Knowing what is happening, and why, can help both the person struggling with their response mechanism and the person who is being perceived as a threat. Don't expect a rational and calm conversation in these moments. Give the threatened person time to recover from the programmed response before you move forward and continue the conversation.

To help protect yourself in a world of psychological rather than physical threats, it is important to pay attention to signals that you get from your body, telling you that you are in fight-or-flight mode. These signals can include muscle tension, increased heartrate, shallow breathing, deep sighing, headaches, or upset stomachs. Symptoms can also appear as feelings of fear, anger, hopelessness, poor concentration, frustration, sadness or even depression. Recognizing the signals means you can examine your environment, identify the perceived threat, and do something about it before you are in full response mode.

As parents and teachers, you will need to recognize and deal with your own moments of negativity and threat, but you also play a large role in the lives of your charges. By avoiding situations where you might unintentionally back children into a corner, you can help avoid this response and its resulting negative emotions.

If the response has already been triggered, don't expect the person you are dealing with to be reasonable, and don't be unduly harsh if they are aggressive. This response is a primitive one that is hardwired into everyone's behavior; they are acting as nature intends them to when survival is at stake.

If you want to have a conversation that gets a point across and has a positive result, aim to create a safe environment where all participants feel comfortable expressing their feelings.

Positive Emotions

Feelings of positivity make us happy, and there aren't many people who stop to ask themselves where those good feelings come from. Now that we know a little about negative emotions, it would be helpful to delve deeper into the purpose of positive ones.

Martin Seligman says positive emotions trigger a 'Here be growth' mindset. This is the time when you are open to learning new skills, making new social connections, and creating new solutions that will help you survive when you perceive danger in a win-lose scenario.

When you are feeling positive, you see yourself in a win-win scenario. You don't feel you need to fight for survival; it is a time of cooperation, rather than competition. When you experience good emotions, you are more open to making new friends and creating lasting relationships. You are more creative, tolerant, and receptive to new ideas and experiences. Not surprisingly, people like you more when you are in a good mood.

I mentioned previously that positivity makes it possible to overestimate your skill-levels. This is known as a positivity bias. It helps you to take risks, try something new, or make new social connections, all important skills for growth.

When I was in school, I was that kid who spent their life trying to avoid physical education. My favourite thing about leaving high school, was not being forced to participate in sporting activities anymore. My dislike didn't come from a lack of fitness, or a fear of being seen in gym shorts, it came because I believed I had absolutely no skill for any type of sport. I couldn't throw or catch a ball, or hit it further than a few inches with a field hockey stick; in short, I was useless at any sporting skill that existed.

When I was in my mid twenties, I was socializing with some friends when someone asked me to join their slow-pitch softball team. I did aerobics classes regularly and was relatively fit. Surely, I couldn't be as bad at throwing and catching as my memory seemed to indicate. I'd been worried that I'd embarrass myself when I was in high school. Now that I was older, I'd be fine.

It is important to understand that I was in a social situation when this request was made. I was laughing with friends, and feeling good about life. For a reason that I didn't understand until I started learning about emotions, I agreed. As I reread these sentences, I am shaking my head. What was I thinking?

What caused me to have a complete about-face in attitude towards sports, and to think I had suddenly discovered a natural talent that had simply lain dormant? Feeling positive made me overestimate my abilities, feel willing to take a risk, and try something I would never have done if I wasn't feeling so happy.

When you are feeling positive, you can benefit from believing you are better than you are. With this surge in confidence you are much more likely to try something new or be bold in social interactions.

In Barbara Fredrickson's paper on the function of positive emotions, she suggests that optimistic emotions allow you to learn new skills and increase your physical, intellectual, and social resources. These resources are then available for you to draw on when you feel threatened and need these skills to survive.

Did I discover a hidden ability to play softball? No! I was as bad as I had ever been. After trying me out in several different positions, the team decided I should play back catcher. If anyone was running towards Homeplate, the first baseman would run Home to catch the ball. The fact that I let every single pitch go past me and had to run to retrieve the ball, then hand it to the pitcher who had walked over from the mound because the chance of me being able to throw it to him was little-to-none, still embarrasses me to this day.

My positive emotions gave me the courage to take a risk and try something new, but the first ball I missed that day brought my insecurities and negative emotions back. These emotions caused me to realistically assess my ability, and deprived me of the frame of mind I needed to learn the skills necessary to play slow-pitch.

Did I persevere? No! After a couple of practices and one game, I resigned from the team. My feelings of optimism had turned sour, and I was back to my previous thoughts and behaviours when it came to sports. My negative emotions and my mindset ensured that I continued to believe I had been born with no sporting ability and that there was no way of changing that.

Emotional Contagion

Emotional contagion is the phenomenon of having the emotions of one person trigger similar emotions and behaviors in the people around them. If you have ever worked with someone who is constantly negative and complaining, you may have seen this in action. Before you know it, everyone in the office is feeling disgruntled and dissatisfied. Research shows that both positive and negative emotions spread between people like a super-virus.

Some people are more susceptible than others to catching the moods of people around them. These people are more likely to feel rapid shifts in emotions as they engage in different social interactions.

Studies have discovered that negative emotions are usually more infectious that positive ones, perhaps because humans react more strongly to bad things than to good. In primitive times, finding food and avoiding predators were both vitally important to survival, but for the most part, the need to escape danger was more necessary than the need for food. You could probably miss a meal or two, but you couldn't afford to be caught by a predator. If humans were drawn more strongly to food than to the avoidance of danger, we might not be here now.

Once you recognize that you have picked up someone else's negative mood, try distancing yourself from the person, or try to counter their bad emotions with good ones. For each negative statement they make, try smiling broadly, or saying something positive.

If you are the person whose mood is negatively affecting others, being aware of this is a useful thing to recognize. It can provide you with a good reason to change your mood or give other people some space until you can ride the negative emotions out.

Understanding Emotions

You need both positive and negative moods in your life. The bad times make it easier to appreciate the good ones, but more than that the good times prepare you with skills and connections that you can use to your advantage during tougher moments. Both types of emotions are necessary for you to live a full life.

Creating a safe and secure environment is essential for learning. This goes for both educational and home settings. Emotional responses happen before cognitive understanding kicks in; when threatened, you act without thought. This is an essential understanding to have when you interact with others.

If you feel threatened in any way, your instincts will cause you to withdraw to what you know and prevent you from learning new skills. As teachers and parents, it is vital that you create classrooms, schools, and homes that foster feelings of safety and acceptance, ensuring that every person who enters it feels free from threats. This takes energy, determination, and conscious effort. Strategies and suggestions on how to do this are included in section three, so make sure you read on.

Perception

After upsetting my husband once in the early days of our marriage, I apologized, only to be told that I didn't really mean it. I did mean it, and for whatever reason I felt it was necessary to convince him that I really was sorry. It led to a long argument that accomplished nothing.

This isn't an uncommon occurrence, nor was it the only time I was involved in that type of situation – both on the giving and receiving ends of the conversation. I'm mentioning this only because it is a good example of perception. I really was sorry for what I had said, but from my husband's viewpoint, I was just saying it without any genuine feeling of regret.

Watching my parents share a memory is always entertaining. My father usually starts the story only to have my mother interject to correct the parts she thinks he has told incorrectly. After this goes on for a certain length of time, my dad asks my mom if he was there during the event, because he doesn't recall the story she is telling at all.

Again, this is a common situation; the way you perceive an event can be very different from the way another person does. Add the complexity of memory into the mix and you have a powder keg ready to ignite.

Perception is the way you interpret the words, actions, and non-verbal signals that you encounter from other people. The way you perceive a situation is not necessarily the same as the way they perceive it. I may make a comment to my husband, who interprets what I am saying as unnecessarily aggressive, while in my head I'm speaking in a conversational tone. Who is right in situations like these? The answer all depends on your perception. It's like the term 'subjective well-being.' Everyone has their own interpretation.

In the world of positive psychology, feelings and emotions are subjective and perception is king. How a person perceives a situation – and the emotions that accompany it – is the way it will affect them. You may worry that your son doesn't have enough friends, but if your son thinks he has lots of friends then all is well. His perception is the deciding factor. Believing you have friends means you will benefit from the positive feelings those friendships bring. It doesn't matter what anyone else thinks.

When you are modelling happiness, you need to keep the idea of perception in the front of your mind. If someone honestly thinks you are being unfair, that is the emotion they will be experiencing, and that is the feeling they need to deal with. It doesn't matter if you agree with them or not.

Often arguments and communication problems come from a difference in perception. Keep communication open and be willing to accept other people's feelings as valid, even if you don't agree with them. Valuing another person's feelings is a great starting point for moving forward.

Hedonic Adaptation

As a teenager, I went to a weekend conference in Prince George, British Columbia where one of the major industries is pulp and paper. After driving for nine hours, I was more than ready to reach our destination – until we arrived. As I climbed out of the car, the first thing I noticed was the smell. As a sixteen year-old, I wasn't programmed for tolerance, and I would gladly have got back in the car and driven nine more hours to get home and away from the smell if someone had offered. But no one did, and my only choice was to breathe through my mouth and hope that time went quickly.

As the weekend progressed, I forgot to breathe through my mouth and became less concerned about the smell. It wasn't until it was time to leave that it struck me that I didn't notice it anymore. Even when I took a deep breath in, I could barely discern the odor that had seemed unbearable only a few days earlier.

Please don't let this story deter you from visiting Prince George. I was there for work a few years ago and had to wonder if I had been imagining the smell. Upgrades to the mills have improved the situation immensely.

This story is an example of the astonishing capacity humans have to adapt to new situations. Think about jumping into a lake or pool. Your first reaction might be 'this is too cold,' but if you stay in the water for a few minutes, your body soon gets used to it.

You adapt not only to physical conditions, but also to emotional ones.

Brickman, Coates and Janoff-Bulman conducted a study to compare the perceived happiness levels of lottery winners, before and after their windfall. They discovered that after an initial burst of increased happiness, the participating lottery winners returned to their pre-winning level of happiness.

Many studies have been conducted to explore the idea of hedonic adaptation. You have a range of happiness that is 'normal' for you, and regardless of the emotional highs and lows that happen in your life, you will return to your set-point range of happiness. This is very much like the thermostat in your house. As the air heats up or cools down, the temperature control starts the furnace or air conditioner to ensure everything remains the appropriate temperature.

In the section on the importance of emotions, I introduced you to Martin Seligman's phrase 'Here be growth' to describe the state you are in when you are experiencing positive emotions. The contrasting term he used to describe the state of negative emotions is 'Here be dragons.' Let me add a third term to the mix. I call this state 'Here be complacency' and use it to describe your emotions when you are feeling an extreme level of happiness. You might feel this way when you initially find out you are a millionaire, get engaged, buy the house of your dreams, get the promotion you've been working towards for five years, or any other change of circumstance that you perceive as the perfect thing to make you happy. When you are in this 'over the moon' level of happiness, you no longer feel an urge to grow and improve. You just want to stand still and enjoy the sensation.

Stop for a moment and think about the three states: feeling negative emotions due to perceived danger, feeling positive and ready to learn new things, or feeling ecstatically happy and just enjoying what seems to be the perfect moment in life. Which one of these is the optimum state for you to spend most of your time in?

If you said the growth state, you agree with the experts. If you get good news and then spend the rest of your life in a state of euphoria, you wouldn't be learning, growing, and progressing. In evolutionary terms, you wouldn't be putting yourself in a good place for continued survival. If you stayed permanently in the negative state of being hunkered down, preparing for danger, you also would not grow or move forward.

The best place to invest your time is in the mildly-to-moderately happy state, where you are confident, open to new experiences, and ready to make social connections. Hedonic Adaptation pulls you down when you become so happy that you grow complacent about life, and then swoops in like a super hero to pull you up when you nose-dive into a negative state. This is the reason your life is so full of ups and downs. It can be reassuring to know this is a natural cycle that everyone experiences; you aren't being singled-out.

When you notice your extreme happiness has faded away, don't be sad. Understand that your brain is ensuring your continued survival. When life gets tough and you find yourself in a dark place, rest assured that those feelings won't last forever; hedonic adaptation will ensure you always come back to your normal, or near normal, level of happiness.

Your Equation for Happiness

$G + C + IA = H$

Genetics + Circumstance + Intentional Activity = Happiness

Research has identified genetics, circumstance and intentional activity as the variables that make up your individual level of happiness. Your happiness isn't one specific point; it is a range of feelings that are normal for you.

Genetics

Genetics encompass all the traits you inherited from your parents: 50% from your biological mother and 50% from your biological father.

Your emotions are affected by neurotransmitters, the brain chemicals that relay messages between neurons. Your genetic code then determines how your brain uses these chemicals, making it one pronounced area where nature can deal you a good hand or a challenging one.

Circumstance

Your circumstance is your environment and how you interact with it. This includes things like your upbringing, your financial situation, and your profession.

Intentional activity

Science refers to intentional activity as the things you think about and then make a conscious decision to do. Circumstance can occur without any input from you, while intentional activity involves acting on circumstance rather than reacting to it.

Nature vs Nurture

Your nature – genetic makeup – and how you were nurtured – your circumstances – work together to decide how happy you are, but which one is more important? Does the person who raises you hold the key to your eventual level of happiness, or are your genes in charge of your level of wellbeing?

The debate over what controls us more, nature or nurture, has been raging for decades. In truth, separating genetics from environmental influences is a difficult task. Life circumstances and genes affect one another to such an extent that it is difficult to tell what has resulted from nature and what has resulted from nurture.

Circumstance probably has more of an effect on your happiness if you are worried about whether you will have enough money to pay your rent and buy food, than when you are confident that you will be provided for.

To add even more confusion, not all inherited traits present themselves. You may have a predisposition for risky behaviour, depression, or alcoholism, but that doesn't mean you will become an alcoholic or be clinically depressed. If the environmental event that sets the gene into motion never shows itself, the gene may remain quietly in the background for the entire span of your life.

As a result, it is difficult to put an exact value on how much your well-being is influenced by nature and how much by nurture. The two things are intertwined to such a degree that it's made an impossible task. Your environment can switch genetic traits on or off, or leave them dormant. Suffice it to say that both factors play important roles in your level of life satisfaction.

One source we have on the genetics vs circumstance contribution to happiness levels comes from David Lykken and Auke Tellegen, who studied 1,300 sets of twins. These studies included identical and same-sex non-identical twins. They looked at twins who were raised together and at those who were separated at birth and raised in different environments.

These studies showed that all the life events or circumstances of one identical twin made little difference when they were compared to the other twin. The level of happiness in identical twins, even if they were raised separately, was very similar. This was the case even if one twin was assessed when they were twenty and the other one when they were thirty. In other words, if identical twins are raised in totally different circumstances, they will still have a similar level of happiness. This evidence points to a strong genetic component in your life satisfaction.

Not all Variables are Equal

If there are mathematicians reading this, please forgive me for the inaccuracy of the Happiness Equation I showed you. It is inaccurate, because not all of the variables have the same weighting. The equation should look more like this:

$$G * 5 + C + IA * 4 = H$$

To make the equation clearer, let's turn it into a pie chart.

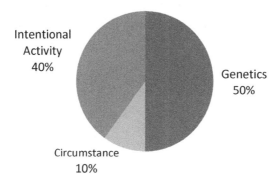

If you look at the graph, it's easier to see that science believes up to 50% of your happiness comes from your genetics, about 10% from your circumstance, and approximately 40% from intentional activity.

If you believe that simply improving your circumstances will lead to long-term happiness, this information is here to burst that bubble. It doesn't matter how much you buy or achieve, in the end it's going to make very little difference to how happy you feel over an extended period of time.

Think back to the theory of Hedonic Adaptation. Any circumstances that send your happiness levels soaring will affect you only temporarily before your mood is pulled back down, so you can return to a level that is conducive to growth. Changing your circumstance will not leave you with a long-term happiness high.

You do, however, have the power to change your level of happiness in a significant way, despite your genetics and your circumstances, if you turn your efforts towards intentional activity. This is the one variable that you have true control over, and it is responsible for at least 40% of your positive feelings.

If you are given a surprise test at school and you didn't get an opportunity to study, that is circumstance beyond your control. What you decide to do because of this circumstance is your intentional activity. You can choose to complain about how unfair the teacher is, or you can take your results and work on the things you didn't know so you are ready for the next exam.

Certain intentional activities have been proven to boost your level of positivity. Examples of such activities include goal setting, doing kind things for others, surrounding yourself with positive people, and taking care of yourself physical, socially, and mentally.

Motivation

When I started teaching elementary school, I felt I knew all the important skills about being a good teacher. But one thing it hadn't prepared me for was the feeling of not being needed. I can remember a social studies lesson near the end of the school year when I looked up and realized that every student was totally absorbed in what they were doing. There was a wonderful buzz in the air as the groups of students at each activity station helped each other and discussed the best approach to complete the activities.

I remember thinking, 'What do I do now? They don't need me!' It was a strange feeling, because I had never thought about my role as a teacher involving creating independent students. At first, the discovery concerned me, but I grew to realize that leading children to become engrossed in their education was essentially what I was working towards.

There is nothing more satisfying than watching someone who is totally absorbed in learning, or practicing a new skill. Some people fall into this behavior naturally, while others struggle and never seem engrossed in acquiring different knowledge and abilities.

Science has provided some useful information to help create an environment that encourages students of all ages to become actively involved in learning. If you want to avoid discipline problems in your classroom, make sure you take appropriate steps to motivate your students. Bad behavior often comes from a lack of belief and interest.

Traditionally, psychologists believed that there were only two reasons for motivation: biological and incentive-driven. We eat because we are hungry (biological) and we work hard at school to earn good grades (incentive).

In 1949, a professor of psychology at the University of Wisconsin named Harry F. Harlow began an experiment on learning. The research involved eight rhesus monkeys. To prepare them for a study that would examine their problem-solving ability, he created a simple mechanical puzzle, and placed several of them in the monkeys' cages to see what they would do. Harlow was surprised to see that, without any encouragement, the monkeys began to play with the puzzles. He was even more amazed to observe that they seemed to be enjoying the activity.

They very quickly figured out how to solve the devices and did so over and over. This didn't fit with either of the previously known motivations. The monkeys had no biological need to solve the puzzles, nor were they being offered any incentive. This unexpected behaviour led Harlow to suggest a third reason for motivation: intrinsic reward. In other words, the monkeys solved the puzzles simply because they were rewarded with positive feelings; they enjoyed finding the solution.

If you have ever taken a psychology course, you have probably learned about extrinsic and intrinsic motivation. Extrinsic, or external, refers to motivation that comes from external factors that include rewards, evaluations, and bonuses. It can be positive or negative. You may work hard to earn good grades (positive), or to avoid a parental lecture (negative). Both are examples of extrinsic motivators. Intrinsic refers to internal motivation, like doing something because it makes you or someone else happy.

The Self-determination Theory

In 1968, Edward Deci, who was then a psychology graduate student, began to look for a dissertation topic. He stumbled across Harlow's research and became interested in carrying it further. Richard Ryan joined Deci, and together they created the self-determination theory. This model suggests there are three human needs that must be satisfied in order for you to feel motivated: competence, autonomy, and relatedness.

Competence is believing that you can do things well enough to be successful; autonomy is the belief that you have at least some control over the things you do; and relatedness is perceiving that you have bonds with the people around you. If you want your students or children to be motivated at school, make sure they believe they have the ability to learn, have at least some degree of control over their schooling, and feel connected to the school community.

It is important to note that it's the child's perception that determines whether any or all of these needs have been satisfied. *They* must believe they have achieved competence, autonomy, and relatedness for the need to be satisfied. If you haven't already read the section on perception, I suggest you do so. It is an important factor in the discussion of human behavior.

As a teacher or parent, you need to communicate with your students and family to establish how they see things. You can't just create opportunities for others to achieve autonomy and assume that the need has been satisfied. If your student doesn't believe they have competence, autonomy, and relatedness, then they don't. Using the power of the self-determination theory relies wholly on perception.

A Warning about Incentives

We live in a world of incentives; we believe children will excel if we reward them for a good report card, and employees will work harder if we promise them a bonus. Harlow's research went deeper than just exposing a new type of motivation. It also revealed some intriguing information about incentives.

Harlow believed that internal motivation would be less important than biological needs or incentives, so he withheld food for twenty-two hours from several of the monkeys who had been playing with the puzzles. He then showed the hungry animals that he was putting food into the puzzles, before placing them into their cages. He thought they would quickly open the familiar devices to get to the food as quickly as possible, but instead of flawlessly solving the puzzles like they had many times before, the monkeys made more mistakes. Once the puzzles were opened and the food eaten, they showed no further interest in them. The enjoyment the puzzles had once held no longer appeared to exist.

The scientific world wasn't ready to take notice of Harlow's research on motivation, so he shifted to another direction with his work. When Deci later uncovered it, he was intrigued and ready to continue developing the discoveries Harlow had made.

Deci created a study using college students and Soma cubes (a puzzle with pieces that can be fitted together to make different shapes). The students were divided into two groups. Being part of the study involved coming into the lab three times and repeating the same process. Each time a participant arrived, he was given some magazines and a soma cube.

During their first visit, all of the students were treated the same way. They were taken into a room and shown a picture of a completed puzzle shape and asked to recreate it themselves. After the student completed several of the shapes, Deci told them he needed to enter their progress into the computer, and that they could do whatever they wanted while he was gone.

Leaving the room to enter the results in the computer was not a strange thing to do in 1968, as computers at that time were large enough to occupy an entire room. But Deci had no intention of entering results into a computer. Instead, he went into the next room and observed what the student did during this free time.

During their first visit, when all the students were treated the same way, they tended to spend their free time continuing to play with the puzzle. They seemed to enjoy creating new shapes. This is the behavior that was observed each time for those who were part of group B, the students that participated each time with no expectation of reward.

On the second visit, those who were part of group A were told they would be paid for each shape they could create. During their free time, they busied themselves with the puzzles, as if to get in more practice so they could make more money. This fits perfectly with the common beliefs held around the power of incentives.

The third time the members of group A came to the lab, they were told that there was no more money, so they would not be paid for each shape they made in that session. When they found out this news, these students seemed to lose interest in the puzzles during their free time and turned to the magazines. By contrast, the members of group B continued to play with the puzzles during the free time of all three sessions. Their interest in them remained constant.

Deci concluded that not only were incentives short-term

solutions, they were capable of damaging internal motivation. This theory was tested with other studies that yielded similar results. Humans seem to be programed to feel that, once you've been rewarded for something, why should you do it just for fun?

This is a drastically different idea for many parents, as well as the education and business worlds, who believe the way to motivate is to offer extrinsic rewards. How many of you have offered, or have been offered, money or other incentives for good grades at school or a strong performance at work? The research shows this isn't a good idea if you want intrinsic motivation to encourage engagement.

If you give your children an allowance, don't link it to specific tasks. Learning to manage money is important, but give it regardless of whether the children get their work done or not. By not linking money and chores, you will help keep their internal motivation for helping around the house intact.

The Needed Nine

Peter Warr introduced the world to the 'Needed Nine' features for happiness in his publication, *Work, Unemployment, and Mental Health*. These features identify the nine main external sources of happiness and unhappiness in any area of your life. They are:

1. Personal influence

    Having at least some level of perceived autonomy or control over what is happening to you. No one wants to be micromanaged, or to feel they are at the mercy of the world around them without any ability to influence their life.

2. Using your abilities

    People need opportunities to apply their skills, to do what they are good at and get better at it. This doesn't mean that you should only do what you are good at, but having chances to use existing skills to achieve goals and solve problems is important for self confidence.

3. Demands and goals

    You need to be required to do specific tasks if you want to be happy. It's like having purpose and a reason to get up in the morning. Often, we create goals for ourselves, but research shows we need our environment to set demands and goals that require us to take action and work through challenges we wouldn't necessarily choose for ourselves.

4. Variety

This is the 'spice of life,' and research backs up that old saying. You can quickly fall into familiar patterns and habits, but getting stuck in one place and repeating the same thing over and over can cause negative emotions. Humans resist constant repetition.

5. Clear requirements and outlook

Being uncertain about what is expected and what your future holds can cause anxiety, even for risk-takers. Research has repeatedly shown that it is difficult to be happy if you are uncertain about what to do, or are unable to predict the result of your actions. Both are necessary aspects to making reliable decisions.

6. Social contacts

Humans are social creatures and without interaction and friendships it is difficult to feel happy. Being part of a team is essential for a happy home or school. You will use these contacts to understand yourself better, and have a clearer perspective of the world around you.

7. Money

This isn't an element that necessarily affects children, but it can if they are aware of their parents' worry about paying the bills and putting food on the table. If you don't have enough money to be adequately cared for, then money will affect your level of happiness. That said, anyone who thinks winning the lottery will make them happy is sadly mistaken. Once you have enough money that you no longer need to worry about paying the rent, or feeding and clothing your family, increased money will not make you happier. Many rich people are woefully lonely and unhappy.

8. Adequate physical setting

   As well as having the basic amenities to live and learn, your environment needs to offer you a place where you feel safe from danger. Schools, classrooms, and homes need to provide safe havens for the people who reside there, if they want them to be conducive for learning.

9. A valued role

   Being valued, or doing something you perceive as making a difference for others, is an important element of happiness. As a teacher, you can boost your job satisfaction by viewing what you do as guiding the next generation of leaders and change-makers, rather than showing up to your classroom just for the money. Parents who take a similar view of their role in the family will share in that boost of happiness.

   Children also need to see what they are doing as valuable - either for themselves, or as a helper for others in the school or wider environment.

Section III –
The Precepts

Introducing the Precepts of Robust Happiness

In this section, you will learn about the eight precepts of robust happiness. A precept is a principle for action. Learning is important, but having knowledge alone won't lead to change. You need to take that information and act upon it if you want to create transformation.

You will find there is a good deal of overlap between the precepts. They link tightly together, so as you add one into your life you will discover elements of other ones being added along with it. One action step may encourage the addition of several different precepts. Utilizing these precepts will help you build happiness that can survive challenges, and will help you remain mentally strong throughout your life.

Remember that the best way to help others is to model the elements and talk about them openly. If you are modelling a happy life, you will be more successful in inspiring others to do the same. Think back to the sad statistics from mental health organizations world-wide; we can't afford to let this situation go unchecked.

Your children may look happy and well-adjusted, and hopefully they are, but bear in mind the number of silent sufferers that exist. Everyone needs to be equipped to take responsibility for their own happiness, and it's up to all of us to make sure children have the tools and information they need to create a life of robust happiness.

Precept #1
Enjoy the Journey

What do you picture when you think of yourself living a happy life? Do you imagine having bad hair days, and feeling frustrated with your family? I suspect most people see themselves in a world without negative emotions and annoyances. Having lots of money and being able to retire from your job may be among the top scenarios that pop into your mind.

If you stop to consider the purpose of your emotions, you will realize that life is designed to contain good times and bad ones. It isn't realistic to expect to be happy during every waking minute of the day. The aim for robust happiness is simply to experience more positive emotions than negative ones.

You live in an ever-changing environment that you have little control over. It isn't the challenges that make you unhappy, it is the way you deal with them. There is nothing more exhilarating than encountering a difficulty and triumphing over it. Those tough times result in many of the most enjoyable experiences of life.

Although our society promotes the idea of achieving never-ending happiness, it isn't reality, and if you believe it is, you are destined to be disappointed. Chasing happiness is a lot like pursuing a butterfly; just as you get close to it, it flutters off to a plant slightly further ahead. Even if you do manage to catch happiness, hedonic adaptation (see The Science Behind the Precepts) exists to ensure that you soon return to your set-point level of well-being.

Having boosts of positive feelings give you the push you need when you have new or difficult tasks to complete. Enjoy these emotional highs, but be aware that they won't – and shouldn't – last forever. After all, if you felt ecstatic all the time, you would be less likely to move forward and adapt to the changes in your environment.

Lead author Jason Riis decided to compare the happiness levels of a group of healthy individuals with a group of dialysis patients. Each participant was asked to carry a Palm Pilot for a week. These devices would beep every ninety minutes; when they did, each participant chose the word (pleased, joyful, anxious, and unhappy) that most closely described how they were feeling at that moment. Findings showed that the renal disease patients were just as happy as the healthy people.

A study of breast cancer surgical patients found that most of them felt their lives had been changed for the better in the period of one month to five years after their cancer surgery. I've met numerous people who have changed their view of life completely after experiencing a brush with death. They have a sudden epiphany of what is truly important and what makes them happy. Dreams of retirement rarely have anything to do with it. It becomes more important to enjoy the experiences you are having now, because there is no guarantee that the point in the future you're concentrating on will ever arrive.

The first precept for creating robust happiness is to accept that the joy of life is in the journey you take, rather than in attaining a specific goal, or reaching a desired destination. Focus is important, but if you focus so hard on an event in your future that you take no notice of what is already happening in your life, you are missing out on opportunities to enjoy what you have around you.

George and Laura had worked hard for their entire adult lives. They chose to save as much money as possible to put towards their retirement and their focus was on doing that as early as possible. They put off taking holidays and enjoying some of their hard-earned funds, all to enhance their lives in the years to come. They reached their chosen retirement ages and left work with a smile and a heart full of adventure and expectation.

Two months into their new lifestyle, George was diagnosed with early onset dementia. The life he and Laura had been focusing on for decades was suddenly transformed from a time of enjoyment to one of uncertainty.

Practice Consciousness

Have you ever travelled home from work, only to realize that you've arrived but have no recollection of how you got there? This isn't uncommon, and illustrates how you can go through life without taking note of the people and experiences around you.

How often have you heard people talking about 'the little things' that make them the happiest, or the 'last straw' that breaks them? Often the big things are a result of many small ones.

More than one person has been caught completely off guard when discovering that their partner is miserable and planning to leave their relationship. They may have been unhappy for years without their significant other having any idea of how they were feeling. This is the type of thing that happens when you aren't living in the moment. You don't notice what is happening around you, often because your eyes are firmly fixed on a future event or goal.

Take time to enjoy the experiences you are having right

now, at this moment, rather than focusing on what the future may or may not bring. That isn't to say that you should ignore the future. Setting goals and having dreams is very important, but don't be too regimented on the path you take to get there, and don't focus so intently on your goals that you tune out everything that is happening in the present moment. You can't get back the precious early days with your children if you miss them as they happen.

Mindfulness is a hot topic, and there is good reason for it. Being fully present in the moment allows you to enjoy the experiences life offers. Boost your happiness by practicing living in the moment. Take time to enjoy your day; move your focus from the endpoint to the now.

The Serenity Prayer

God grant me the serenity to accept the things I cannot change;
Courage to change the things I can,
And wisdom to know the difference

One of the hardest things about enjoying the journey is learning to accept that many things you encounter are out of your control. It is a waste of your time and energy to attempt to alter something that can't be changed. For example, as hard as you try, you can't make another person change their mind unless *they* choose to do it. *You* can't decide for them.

Goal Setting

Although you must be cautious about focusing exclusively on your future, you can't completely ignore it either. You need to have an idea of where you are heading. Imagine going on a holiday with absolutely no idea of the destination. How will you know when you arrive? I'm aware there may be some free spirits reading this that think spontaneity is the only way to travel, but bear with me. If you have a limited amount of time before you need to be home, some form of plan is likely to exist, regardless of how fluid it is.

Setting goals has strong links to happiness and satisfaction. Research shows the critical factor when creating goals is the pursuit of them, not necessarily in attaining them. This supports the theory that your joy is in the journey you take, not always where you end up. You don't have to write a goal in stone; writing it in the sand, where it can easily be modified, will make you just as happy. That doesn't mean, however, that you can set a goal to lose weight and then sit back and munch on potato chips. It's the effort you put into reaching your goals that makes you happy. Setting goals you have no intention of working towards, will not boost mood.

Viewing happiness as a trek rather than a destination fits well with goal creation. It may help to think of your goals as milestones, or lights along your path of life. Reaching each goal is not the end of the adventure; enjoy your success, and then set a new goal and continue on your way. Each milestone gives proof that you are moving forward, and helps you believe that because you reached this goal, you can reach the next one.

Try not to feel disappointed if your travels take you to a different place than you had originally intended. Remember that more happiness enters your life while you are working towards a goal than when you actually achieve it. As you deal with unexpected dips and bumps in the road, you learn more about yourself and your environment. Being able to adapt when your path takes an unexpected detour is an important skill to develop.

Maintain a Flexible Approach

The ability to adapt and change with your environment makes good evolutionary sense, both for your distant ancestors and for you today.

It is important to have a flexible attitude towards life, as things rarely unfold exactly to plan. Being adaptable is a necessity, because your environment and circumstances are constantly changing. To survive and thrive, you need to evolve as the things around you do. Standing still is not an option.

Being adaptable was not a natural behavior for me; it was something I had to learn. My parents modelled a certain level of resistance to unexpected change, so that was the way I faced detours as I entered my adult life. With lots and lots of practice, I have become better at being adaptable, but it is still something I have to consciously work on.

Avoid being Judgemental

I grew up in a family of people who loved to have an opinion about the choices and decisions other people made. Because my parents believed the way they chose to live their lives would also serve my siblings and me best, they could be very negative about choices we made that they didn't agree with. When met with this sort of resistance, it can be difficult to stay strong. I was very aware of the choices my parents felt would be good for me, although they weren't necessarily the same ones I wanted to make. This is a struggle many children experience as they grow up.

I have worked hard as an adult to avoid judging other people's decisions, and hope they are able to extend me the same courtesy. I don't know the exact details of the journey anyone is taking but my own, and I don't know what choices I would make if I was living a different life. It's easy to think you know how you would react in a given situation, but as I have matured, I realize that no one really knows what they would do until they are actually in that situation.

Standing in judgement of others is one of the most damaging acts you can commit. Think about how you feel when another person judges your decisions. Do you feel they have a right to do so? This can be an extremely difficult skill for parents to learn, because you want the best for your children and believe you know more. Whether or not you do is unimportant. We all need to learn to make our own way through life if we are going to be happy. Give advice and support, but accept the choices others make as part of their learning experience.

The Principle

You are programed to experience a variety of feelings throughout your life; you can't be happy all the time. Use this knowledge to build a life that has more good than bad in it. Accept challenges and low times, knowing you will feel happy again. Hedonic adaptation will make sure of that.

Everyone has their own journey to take; they alone really know the intricacies of that trek. Guide when necessary, give advice when asked for, but don't take control of someone else's life with the mistaken belief that you know what is best for them.

You learn more when things don't work out as you expected. It keeps you adaptable, and gives you opportunities to develop new skills.

Allow children to fail and learn. Help them recover, and

look for valuable lessons, but don't think it is better for them to only experience success. Learning to deal with failure is a necessary skill for any robustly happy person.

Avoid judging the decisions other people make. Remind yourself they are on their own journey, and it is important for them to take control of it. Accepting that not everyone is like you is one of the most important principles for your happiness, and for the happiness of your loved ones and students.

Action

1. Learn about the purpose of your emotions

    Increase the enjoyment you have on your journey by understanding how emotions work and the purpose behind them. Becoming aware of the fight-or-flight response and hedonic adaptation can make it easier to accept the ups and downs life presents.

2. Live in the moment

    Be mindful of what is happening currently in your life, rather than focusing too heavily on the future. Use some of the following strategies to help you appreciate the present moment:

    a. Practice meditation
    b. Take time to drink in the sights and smells that surround you
    c. Examine, draw, or photograph something in your environment
    d. Keep a journal and reflect on your day: what went well, what are you grateful for, what could you have done

differently

e. Every morning, before you get out of bed, set an intention for your day

    i. Stop periodically during the day to remind yourself of your intention

    ii. At the end of the day, reflect on whether it turned out as you planned

3. Enjoy the entire journey

When you go on a field trip or holiday, begin the experience as soon as you leave the front door. Challenge your companions to find interesting sights and sounds on the way to and from your destination.

4. Become a people watcher

Observe the choices and decisions made by others, but don't attach judgement to them. You can learn a lot by watching the people around you.

5. Accept others as they are

This doesn't mean you have to like every person who crosses your path, but grant them the courtesy of living their own life and learning their own lessons. Don't expect everyone to be just like you. Model accepting, non-judgemental behavior.

6. Try to be resilient when you feel others are judging the decisions you have made

Practice being strong when you feel you are being judged.

Remind yourself of the importance of taking charge of your life. If you made a considered choice based on what you thought was best at that moment in time, then it was the right choice for you. If it didn't work out the way you wanted, look for a lesson and learn from the experience. You will be richer for it.

7. Be a guide for the journeys that your students and children take

Teach others the importance of being responsible for their own journeys. Help them understand that life contains both good times and challenging ones, and that they will learn more from the difficult situations. Offer insight and comfort, but let them make their own way.

8. Share your experiences with others

Knowing that other people go through the same problems that you do can be wonderfully comforting. More importantly, if you talk with others that have been in similar situations, you can learn from their experiences. As a happiness model, it is important to start a conversation about emotions, and the challenges you face, allowing others a place to talk about *their* emotions and challenges. There is a lot of truth in the old saying, 'A trouble shared is a trouble halved.'

9. Create Goals

Being able to see that you are making progress on your journey is important. These goals are markers along your path, not destinations or endpoints, but they will add to your feelings of positive wellbeing.

Tips for Creating Goals

1. Create goals that can be measured

    If you simply aim to be happier, it can be difficult to know whether or not you're succeeding. You need specific ways to evaluate whether your mood is becoming more positive.

2. List long and short term goals

    Both types of goals contribute equally to boosting your happiness.

3. Be careful who you share your goals and accomplishments with

    Telling someone who failed a performance review that you are employee of the month may be seen as insensitive.

4. When others share their goals with you, be conscious of how you respond

    Positive feelings for a person sharing goals or good news is strongest when the listener responds with a supportive verbal message and non-verbal cues that show genuine pleasure and interest.

5. Keep an achievement diary

    List your accomplishments each day and choose one to reflect on. Think about how it has contributed to your life. Feel proud of what you have done. It may take a month or more to see the effect this activity has on your happiness, but trust me, it will be worth the effort.

6. Shoot for the stars, but don't expect your goals to happen overnight or without hard work and energy

It is better to think the way ahead will require you to dig deep and then be pleasantly surprised if it doesn't, than to think everything will fall into place without a hitch and then be disappointed.

7. Take time to examine your expectations

If they seem high without any concrete reason to feel that way, try to rein them in slightly. If you find yourself disappointed about something that hasn't lived up to your expectations, rather than viewing it as a failure, think about the skills and lessons you learned along the way.

Conclusion

No matter what you do in your life, or what journey you take, you are never going to be happy all the time. You are going to experience both positive and negative emotions. Remind yourself that both states are important for your personal development and survival. Knowing that your life is designed to contain a variety of emotions makes it easier to live through the difficult times.

I believe children should be introduced to the purpose of our emotions from an early age. It is healthy for them to understand that all types of feelings are important and serve a deeper purpose. It helps them not only understand themselves better, but also to understand others.

To create a happier life, find a way to enjoy the journey it takes you on. Learn to observe others without judgement, remembering they too are on a journey of their own.

Precept #2
Create a Mindset for Success

Whether you think you can,
Or think you can't,
You're right.

Henry Ford

Mindset

Mindsets are sets of strong beliefs that you have, which are used to view and evaluate life.

A few years ago, I had the good fortune to stumble onto Carol Dweck's book *Mindset*. I was searching for an interesting audio book to listen to in the car, as I had some long-distance commuting to do for work. The information I heard literally changed my life. I bought a hard copy of the book, as well as having the audio version, so I could highlight important sections. I return to this book repeatedly, and listen to the entire volume at least once a year.

If you haven't read *Mindset*, I highly recommend it. In it, Dweck introduces the reader to fixed and growth mindsets, two very different sets of beliefs on the nature of intelligence and ability.

Fixed versus Growth

People with the fixed mindset believe that intelligence is

predetermined; you come into the world with a certain level of ability that never changes. Geniuses are born, not created. If you are smart, you can do things effortlessly without being taught.

Natural ability is the cornerstone of the fixed mindset. If you are born smart, you will be smart forever without needing to work at it. If you are born without natural abilities, too bad, as that situation will never change. With this mindset, failing means you are a failure, and succeeding means you are a success.

This is the mindset I had for the first three or four decades of my life. I compared myself to my siblings – another trait of the fixed mindset – and found myself lacking. The result of believing I was less talented than my brother and sister meant I shied away from challenges and only did what I knew I could do successfully. I didn't want to prove my family, or myself, right about my lack of intelligence. Not trying meant the feelings I had about my intelligence were only a suspicion, not a proven fact.

Did my fixed mindset parents actually think I was less able than my siblings? Probably, although I doubt they would ever admit this. My brother was three and a half before my sister was born. During those years, my mom spent a lot of individual time with him. He taught himself to read at an early age, and when he was given an IQ test, his score was very high. Remember, one of the beliefs of the fixed mindset is in predetermined ability, so if my brother was bright at age five, he would be bright for his entire life. My parents were as proud as punch.

I was the third child, and very close in age to my older sister. I didn't talk clearly until I was three; if I grunted, my sister would understand what I wanted and do the talking for me. I was a sunny, smiley child, and as I grew up, my parents thought of me as the social one; my siblings were the intelligent ones.

Does any of this sound familiar? Were you raised in a family of fixed mindset people, or are you displaying traits of having a fixed mindset in your own family?

The alternative to having a fixed mindset is having a growth mindset. With this attitude, you believe the intelligence and ability you are born with is just a starting point; with effort and learning you can get smarter. You believe in life-long learning, and are interested in continually finding out more about yourself and the world around you. With a growth mindset, failing at a challenge doesn't label you as a failure. It simply means you can't do that activity – yet. If you practice and learn more, you may be able to do it next time.

You can have a mixture of the two mindsets, or have one at work and another in your personal life. Both attitudes are valid, but possessing a growth mindset is much more valuable if you want to be happy.

Because people with the fixed mindset believe geniuses are born and can naturally do things without trying, this is how they want to appear to others. It is important for them to be seen as effortlessly successful. Getting A's without trying or ever doing homework is an admired quality for those with a fixed mindset. A lot of pressure comes from trying to constantly look smart and naturally talented, and much of your energy is spent preserving that image.

For the fixed mindset person, the only thing worse than others not thinking you're smart is the worry that maybe they're right – maybe you aren't as smart as you thought you were. Remember, this mindset believes intelligence is the result of a roll of the genetic dice; if you aren't smart now, you never were and never will be. If, like my younger self, you have a fixed mindset and you suspect that you are lacking when it comes to natural ability, you don't want to put yourself into situations that might prove this shocking thought to be true.

Students with a fixed mindset are more concerned about appearing to be smart than about learning. In one study, Carol Dweck and her team discovered that when children were asked to record the scores they received on an activity for use in another part of their research, those with a fixed mindset often lied about how well they did, even if they had received a good score.

I have to admit to lying once, for this very reason.

It was in PE 10; we were doing a unit on grass hockey and our mark was based on different skills we should have developed during the unit, one being the ability to drive the hockey ball. Your letter grade for this skill depended on how far you could propel the ball.

I could not for the life of me get the ball past a D distance. Our teacher let those of us who wanted to improve our scores have an opportunity to do that, while the rest of the class played a game. No matter how hard I tried, I could not get that hockey ball past the mark for a D grade.

Finally, in a moment of defiance, I went over to the teacher and said that I had made it to the C marker. I justified my behaviour by saying to myself that I wasn't going to ruin my grade point average because of grass hockey.

My fixed mindset was telling me that I could justify what I had done, even though I hadn't earned it. The grade was more important to me than persevering to learn a new skill and becoming better at grass hockey.

Studies show that students who need to prove themselves

aren't interested in what they did wrong in their tests and assignments, or in trying to learn from the mistakes they make, they are focused solely on the mark they receive. For the fixed mindset student, school is all about looking effortlessly intelligent.

In post-secondary education, fixed mindset students often approach studying as a memorization exercise. If you can remember enough of the printed material, then you should be in a good position to answer test questions correctly. You aren't worried about learning, or understanding the material, only about getting a good grade.

For these students, it is more important to look smart than it is to learn new information or skills. They avoid taking risks that might result in what they perceive to be failure. It is better to get a high grade that you didn't earn, than a low one that suggests to others you aren't smart. For students with a fixed mindset, school is all about proving to others, and themselves, that they really are intelligent.

> *The most pressure I ever felt to get good grades in university was when I was at the top of a class. I didn't want to get pushed off my success pedestal. I made choices for class assignments and projects that would ensure my marks kept me on top, rather than choices that would help me grow as a person, teacher, or learner. I felt it was more important to get a top grade than to have learned something.*

For parents and teachers with fixed mindsets, you too are motivated by the need to prove you are naturally intelligent. You may find yourselves pretending you know the answer to something you have no idea about, or adopting the attitude of always being right. This often presents itself through defensive and aggressive behaviors if anyone suggests there may be an alternative viewpoint to yours, or even that you are mistaken.

For the fixed minded parent, emphasis is put on children being able to do things early, without any instruction. If your child teaches herself to read before receiving any lessons, it proves you gave birth to a genius. Children who need to be taught to read, or who learn at an older age, are obviously less gifted. These parents hold the belief that a child who is advanced when they are a toddler will be advanced in everything they do for the rest of their lives.

Don and Tracy's daughter had reached school age and they needed to consider which school she should go to. The one they lived the nearest to didn't have a particularly high academic record and many of the children who attended it were from families who didn't value education very highly.

They settled on the local school, because they preferred that their child be from one of the better-off families. As they put it, she would do better being a big fish in a small pond than a small fish in a big pond.

Their child did well in school and achieved many academic awards for all her hard work. Their decision was perfectly valid, but their reasoning behind it is a textbook example of fixed mindset parents. It is better to look smart in a group of less academic students, than to be average in a group of geniuses.

With the fixed mindset, it is difficult to receive criticism, no matter how helpful or constructive it is. If anyone points out flaws, you will tend to interpret it as a threat to your ability. This reaction sparks the need to justify and deflect. Things are never your fault. The reason you didn't do well was because of the teacher, the pencil you were using, or the fact that your alarm clock didn't go off even though you know you set it properly.

If you have ever watched reality television like *American Idol*, you will probably recall auditioning hopefuls who became excessively angry when they got turned down. The judges were idiots, the show was rigged and no one involved had any true idea of what good music was. These people are prime examples of individuals with the fixed mindset. You may also notice that these contestants tended to give up when times got tough, rather than persevering and overcoming obstacles.

These behaviors and beliefs are foreign to people with the growth mindset. They believe that someone who is taught to read can read just as well, or even better, than a self-taught early starter if they are compared later in their school careers. Being born with a natural ability may give you a head-start, but it doesn't determine how successful you will be in life, or how smart you will end up becoming.

For students with a growth mindset, school is about learning, rather than appearing to be smart. For adults with this attitude, they accept that learning takes time and effort, and that it continues on for an entire life-time. The don't feel the need to compare ability levels; everyone learns at their own pace depending on how hard they try, and how much they practice.

American Idol contestants with this set of beliefs were more likely to listen carefully to the judges' critiques and to learn from the feedback. Even if the words were harsh, they didn't see the feedback as personal or malicious. With a growth mindset, negative evaluation gives you information you can use in an effort to improve. If the feedback was harsh, growth mindset contestants tended to work twice as hard during the week to knock the socks off the panel during the next episode.

Labels, whether you give them to yourself or receive them from others, make life difficult for people with a fixed mindset.

You are afraid to lose a good label, and you fear deserving a negative one. It is easier to give up rather than risk falling off the top or showing others you deserve to be on the bottom. For those with a growth mindset, good labels reflect the amount of effort you have exerted, and negative ones highlight areas that can be improved. They may think, 'I might be at the bottom now, but if I work hard I can climb to the top.'

Viewing Failure

Fixed mindsets are concerned with avoiding mistakes, because failing at something defines them as a failure. They tend to see the world in terms of win-lose situations. You will probably remember from earlier sections that win-lose scenarios tend to push you toward negative emotions as you prepare to fight or flee. People with fixed mindsets aren't as happy as those with growth ones, because they see so much of their world as being win-lose. They work hard to avoid challenges that they aren't confident they can overcome. For them, if victory isn't assured, then it is better not to take part.

With the growth mindset, you can enjoy what you do, even in the face of adversity. You don't see a lack of success as failure, you see it as an opportunity for learning. Life is more than a series of win-lose scenarios, so you don't shy away from taking risks. You appreciate evaluation that helps you continue to work towards your goals. You don't feel the urge to give up when times get tough; instead you persevere to overcome the problem, knowing that by doing so you are getting smarter and creating stronger neural pathways.

Enjoying Your Journey

It is easier to enjoy your journey with this frame of mind guiding your way, because you aren't concerned with what other people will think if they see you working hard or falling short of your goal.

Your mindset affects the way you move through life in a very profound way. With the fixed mindset, you want to protect your perceived level of intelligence and constantly try to prove how smart you are. Rather than concentrating on learning, you concentrate on proving you are already intelligent.

I've moved away from the fixed mindset I had in the first part of my life, and have worked hard to develop a growth one, although there are times when I fall back into old habits. I believe that a person's true potential is unknown. You may have done something wondrous at a young age without any training, but imagine what you could achieve with passion, effort, and learning. As a person who didn't talk much until I was three, I am relieved to think that early performance doesn't determine future success.

Changing Your Mindset

It is possible to change your mindset if you choose, because it involves changing your mind, and that is something we have all done before. Sometimes it takes another person proving to us that we can learn a skill we aren't naturally good at before we start to believe this is possible.

I was convinced that I had no athletic ability, and with my fixed mindset, I believed that would never change. I avoided physical education whenever I could, and when I couldn't wiggle my way out of it, I put as little effort as possible into whatever activity we were doing. No need to prove to everyone that even if I tried I was useless.

I married into a family of tennis players. Everyone played at a competitive level, and I worried that I wasn't going to fit in. My father-in-law taught PE at a young offenders' institute, and he didn't believe that I could be as bad as I claimed.

In an effort to get him to stop bugging me about playing tennis, I let him give me a lesson. I was pretty sure that one visit to the tennis court would be more than enough to get my point across.

My father-in-law is a truly gifted tennis coach. He started me off with skills that were so easy even I could succeed, like bouncing a ball directly to me so I could catch it. Then he bounced the balls a little further away so I had to move my feet. Each and every moment of the lesson was designed to give me success. I didn't always catch the ball, or hit it with my racquet, but we always ended every skill we practiced on 'a good one.'

When we finished my first lesson, I couldn't wait for the next one. I was hooked. For the first time in my life, I had experienced improvement in a physical activity. I might not have been born with a natural affinity for sports, but that didn't mean that I couldn't develop some skills. A seemingly simple lesson, but one that took me almost thirty years to figure out.

You may view your fixed mindset as something that has served you well so far, so why should you change? If it worked for you, why shouldn't it work for your students and family? Regardless of how successful you may view life with a fixed mindset, imagine what it could have been like with a growth one.

Children learn from the role models in their lives. If you

want to make a difference and give them the best chance possible to be mentally healthy throughout their lives, developing a growth mindset is important.

Do you recognize yourself as having characteristics from both mindsets? Do you display different mindsets in different areas of your life? This is very possible. It isn't an all-or-nothing situation.

In my family, it was important to be right, because if you weren't you were wrong and that meant the same thing as losing. As you can imagine, there were lots of arguments and struggles to prove we were right.

I carried this attitude into my adult life and married a man who had been raised with the same beliefs.

> *My husband once suggested that I wasn't as smart as him, because I was just a teacher and he was a lawyer. He later claimed he wasn't being serious, but with my mindset I interpreted it as a very serious comment. My intelligence was being questioned. It was a mighty blow to my confidence as I was already worried enough about not being as smart as my siblings.*
>
> *My reaction wasn't pretty. Instead of calmly telling him I didn't agree, I began to rant and rave. It was a total overreaction, because deep down inside, I thought what he said might be true. My fixed mindset kicked into high defensive mode.*

I still remember this event because it left me exhausted and got me thinking about the best way to stop the same situation from happening again. I knew I was reasonably smart, but my fixed mindset ensured that I didn't carry this belief to my core. To protect my image, I decided it was time for my husband and me to end the comparison game. I stopped vocalizing my fixed mindset comments, but my brain still thought them. It took a walk with my children to spark the change that happened at a deeper level.

> *While out for a walk with my two young children, they asked if we could stop and watch the horses in a field. I decided I would take a moment to do a little teaching, and asked my daughter how many horses there were. 'Five,' she replied. The answer was three, so I asked her to count them with me. When we got to three, she pointed to the other side of the field and asked me, 'What about those ones under the tree?' Sure enough, there were two more that I hadn't noticed.*
>
> *I was wrong and my children were right. While struggling to think of a way out of my blunder, I had an ah-ha moment. My kids weren't judging me for being mistaken; they didn't care that I hadn't seen the two horses under the tree. It was okay to be wrong. I decided that next time I would look more closely, be less sure that I was right, and realize that being wrong didn't reflect on who I was as a person. Not seeing two of the horses didn't make me a less loved, or less effective mother.*

Awareness is the first step to any type of transformation. Although I hadn't yet encountered Carol Dweck's book, I became aware that some of the ways I viewed life were no longer serving me well. I wasn't always right, and being wrong was ok. It didn't reflect on my intelligence, or who I was as a person. I think the book *Mindset* affected me so profoundly because it put into words the beliefs I had already begun to develop when I became a mother

With a fixed mindset, you can hear all the lessons and advice others have to offer – you are only competing against yourself, failure is an opportunity to learn, effort is the key to success – but you are unlikely to buy in. Your mindset is still telling you that success involves being better than your competition, effort is only for those who don't have ability, and failing means you are a failure.

The Principle

The beliefs and attitudes you hold form your mindset and determine how you view and evaluate your life and the world around you. If you believe the intelligence and ability you were born with is just a starting point, that you can continue to learn and get smarter throughout your life, you have a growth mindset. With this attitude, you are more likely to be robustly happy as you don't fear challenges, risks, or failure.

The other mindset is a fixed one, and if you have this attitude, you believe that everyone is born with a predetermined amount of intelligence and ability that won't ever change. With this belief, you are more concerned about looking smart than you are about the journey you are taking through life or the lessons you are learning along the way. If you believe you aren't very intelligent, you don't bother to try and improve yourself because you believe there is no point. It is much harder to be robustly happy with a fixed mindset.

Action

1. Illustrate these mindsets using stories and movies

   This is a wonderful way to teach and reinforce understanding of the mindsets. Look for strong characters that succeed through effort and learning and against all the odds, or need to experience something over and over until they learn what they need to. *Seabiscuit* and *Groundhog Day* are good examples.

Caution: One age-old story that most children hear or read is *The Tortoise and the Hare*. The moral of the story is slow and steady wins the race, but how many of us identify with the tortoise, or want to be seen as slow and steady? You need to find stories with characters children feel a bond with. If you have a fixed mindset, you may well see the tortoise as someone who was born with little ability, but had a lucky break that kept him from being a total loser.

Examining the mindsets of characters can be added into English lessons for books you are already planning to read. This involves tweaking some of the questions and activities you use, rather than implementing an entirely new curriculum.

2.   Choose a growth mindset

Once you understand the differences between the two sets of beliefs, you can practice recognizing the one you are displaying. If you want to change it, start by stopping and reframing your thoughts. If you are developing growth mindsets as a school team, or a family unit, you can help one other recognize when you have taken on fixed beliefs.

Practice recognizing mindsets by observing the people you interact with. I'm not suggesting that you become judgemental about the way others view life, or the choices they make; observing the different mindsets can make it easier to notice when you are falling back into a fixed mindset, and lets you take steps to alter your thought patterns. Remember to be an observer, not a judger.

3. See life as an adventure with expected ups and downs

   Look for opportunities to grow from everything that happens on your journey, even the events you have no control over.

4. All change is a choice

   You can't decide that your partner is going to move from one mindset to another if they don't want to. That shouldn't stop you from modelling the growth mindset, or sharing information about its benefits to encourage others to create a happier life.

5. React to report cards with a growth mindset

   When your children come home with their report cards, be more concerned with their effort marks than their letter grades. You can't always be an A student, but you can always try your best. The harder you try, and the more you practice, the smarter and more skilful you will get. If a report card shows a lack of effort, ask your child why, and talk about ways they can remedy the situation.

   Give feedback that encourages a growth mindset by commenting on their achievements, effort, and growth, rather than their intelligence and natural ability. There will be more about this in Precept #3 when I talk about praise.

Conclusion

The way you view your life has a tremendous amount of influence over how happy you feel. Developing a growth mindset will put you in a much better position to feel positive. Rather than believing failing means you are a failure, you see it as an opportunity to learn. Honoring learning and effort are characteristics of robustly happy people.

Your mind needs to be aware of the way you view life and learning before you can change it. As a person who has lived with both types of mindset, I can attest to the benefits of developing the growth attitude. I am a much more even-tempered person without my fixed beliefs, as I don't feel the same need to protect the image I was projecting to the world. I have a new sense of calm that has come from learning not to judge other people or the journeys they are taking. I may not agree with their choices, but if they aren't harming me, other people, or their own physical well-being, who am I to judge?

Discovering Carol Dweck's book and research changed my life. It shattered my way of viewing the world, and left me with a much better vision of myself and the journey I am taking. It is important to develop a mindset that will set you up for a happy and successful life.

Precept #3
Make Decisions & Take Responsibility

Life is full of choices: what to wear, what to eat, what to spend your money on and so forth, yet many people are still uncomfortable when faced with decisions. There are many reasons for this, including a lack of practice, a fixed mindset, and fear of being responsible for a negative outcome.

The Decision-Making Process

Decision-making is a seamless brain process that you are often unaware of. Your brain goes through a complex process of analysis and evaluation when it needs to make a choice. Throughout your waking hours, you are presented with countless opportunities to make decisions. Some you consider and mindfully make, but many happen without any conscious thought.

Taking Responsibility

Responsibility is the flip-side of decision-making. If you make a choice, then you should be willing to assume responsibility for how it turns out. That's easy if you are happy with the outcome, but more difficult if you aren't, especially if your decision affects others.

For people who make rash decisions without considering the possible outcomes, knowing you are responsible for your decisions may help you be a little more deliberate about making them. 'The buck stops here' is a good mantra to have.

However, for those of you who don't want to take responsibility for the outcome of your decisions, becoming a decision-avoidance expert may be your 'go to' strategy.

My family was full of fixed mindsets. This resulted in a lot of arguments, as being wrong meant that you were less smart than the person who was right. It also made decision making a risky business; I was pretty sure there was always a *right* answer, and I wanted to make sure that was the one I chose. Fear of making the *wrong* decision paralysed my ability to decide on anything that involved another person.

How Decision-making Increases Happiness

Autonomy is a feature in both the Self-Determination Theory and the Needed Nine. It is the ability to be independent, self-governing, and to have a freedom of will over your own actions. To feel happy, you need to *perceive* that you can make choices and decisions for yourself.

The rub is accepting that if you make decisions, you also must be responsible for their outcomes. This is easy enough if you are just choosing a flavor of potato chips, but more difficult if you have been offered two jobs and don't know which one to accept.

If you aren't given the opportunity to make decisions as you grow up, suddenly having to do it as an adult can be daunting, or even debilitating. You may avoid making choices, and instead hand the responsibility to a significant person in your life. Even if you don't choose to let someone else make your decisions for you, if you struggle to do it yourself, you may find the option is taken away from you. Many misguided loved ones think they are doing you a favor by assuming the role of decision-maker in your life. If this behavior becomes a habit, it can be difficult for you to take charge again at some point in the future.

Boost the happiness of others, including your students and children, by helping them learn to make choices and live with the consequences. Do this by starting when they are young with small choices, and then increasing the number and importance of their decisions as they mature.

Being micromanaged doesn't make you happy, but suddenly being thrown into the world to govern yourself when you reach the age of majority isn't a good plan either. Start small, and let the skill develop until the person involved is comfortable with both the decision-making process and taking responsibility for its result.

Decisions and the Mindsets

Fixed

When I was growing up and had a predominantly fixed mindset, I was almost paralyzed with fear over deciding anything, especially if it was a decision that affected someone else. Believing that the world was full of win-lose scenarios, the pressure was always on to ensure I was on the winning side.

My friends must have found me a nightmare, because I always left the decision-making up to them. It didn't help that my mother modelled this behavior for me. She, too, was uncomfortable making choices. It wasn't until I got older, and had learned the importance of sharing the decision-making duties with others, that I glimpsed what it must have been like for the people I spent time with. I thought I was being easy-going, but in reality, I was avoiding taking responsibility for a choice that might not be 'the right one.'

If you don't make decisions in your life, you are handing the responsibility to other people who are then in control of the outcome. The reasoning is good if you have a fixed mindset; if you don't make any of the decisions, you don't have to assume any of the blame.

That may be a safe stance to take, but it isn't a healthy one. Making choices and taking responsibility for them in a non-judgemental way is vital to living a mentally healthy life.

People with fixed mindsets have difficulty taking responsibility for decisions that they see as failures, because they feel labelled by the choices they make. If you make a winning decision, you are a winner, but if your decision is a losing one, you must be a loser. Remember, with this mindset, you see the world in terms of winning and losing.

For these people, the best strategy for dealing with decisions that turn out to be bad ones is to blame something or someone else. You missed the shot because your equipment wasn't good enough. You scored poorly on the exam because the teacher put unfair questions on the test that they hadn't covered in class. The fixed mindset strives to ensure that they are not seen as responsible for making a decision that results in failure.

Growth

For people with the growth mindset, making decisions isn't nearly as scary and doesn't need to be avoided. Instead, it becomes a skill that gets better with practice.

When you view failure as an opportunity to learn, you

don't have the same fear about making decisions and taking responsibility for them. What's the worst that can happen if you make a considered choice? It might not work out. If it doesn't work out, you will still have had the opportunity to learn something about yourself and/or the world around you.

Because those with a growth mindset don't live in fear of failure, they are willing to take risks. Every decision you make involves some degree of risk, even if it is just choosing the toppings for your pizza.

If you are living and learning with a growth mindset, you don't worry that you will be viewed as a loser if your choice doesn't work out as you expected. Your ego isn't concerned with being labelled a failure just because you made a poor decision. The choice was a failure, not you.

Children with this viewpoint have a huge advantage over their fixed mindset counterparts. They can explore the world, making choices and being strong enough to take responsibility for them. They know that the decision does not determine who they are as a person.

Validation

Validation is the need for reassurance or approval. Is the decision you made the best one?

Who do you turn to for validation? Do you seek external approval from your family, friends, and colleagues, or do you turn to yourself? If you believe you made the best decision, regardless of what anyone else thinks, then you are relying on internal validation.

This is the type of reassurance you should strive for if you want to live a happier life.

As you make decisions, you may seek validation to

reassure yourself that your decision is a good one. That sounds harmless enough, but when your need for validation from others becomes your primary motivation for the decisions you make, you are no longer taking your own journey through life. Instead, you may find yourself travelling the path that someone else thinks you should take. There are several problems with adopting this approach if you want to lead a life of robust happiness.

Think about Precept #1 of the Modelling Happiness process. Your journey is unique to you; no one else can understand its intricacies like you can. If you want to be happy, you need to take responsibility for that journey. That includes being accountable for your decisions and the results that follow. If you need approval from others before you can move forward, you may not travel the path that is right for you.

When you have a big decision to make, ask other people who you respect and trust for their opinions. Gather information, and then make a decision that feels right for you. Trust that you made a decision that seemed best at that moment in time with the information you had, and don't worry whether other people agree with you. Take responsibility for your decision, knowing that you can learn from the outcome, regardless of what it is.

Validation and the Mindsets

Looking for external validation is common when you have a fixed mindset. You need your decision to be the right one, and gaining validation from others gives you this reassurance. External validation also means that you aren't responsible for the decision that was made if it doesn't turn out as planned; it's someone else's fault you didn't get the desired end-result. A failed choice that someone else told you was a good one means they are the failure, not you. You can see why people with this type of mindset choose to avoid taking responsibility for decisions.

Our society is full of people who follow this pattern of behavior. If you want to see it in action, watch athletes being interviewed after losing an important match or game. If you hear them talking about poor calls by the referees, not feeling well, or other external reasons for their loss, you are probably looking at someone with a fixed mindset. They need to find a reason for their loss that doesn't involve them.

These athletes see themselves in a win-lose scenario; if the fact that they weren't successful reflected on their ability, then they would have to admit to themselves and the world that they were a failure. That is not a viable option, so they find other reasons for playing below their best standard - reasons that don't reflect negatively on them.

Athletes with a growth mindset hate losing just as much, but they can look at the situation and try to learn from it. They have no problem admitting that their opponent was better on the day, or that they simply under-performed. Failing at that moment isn't the same as being a failure.

Superstar contestant Stephen 'tWitch' Boss is a great example of someone with a growth mindset. He auditioned for 'So You Think You Can Dance' three times before he was chosen to become a finalist. He didn't label himself a failure and give up, he took the rejection as a sign that he needed to keep practising, which he did.

A poor workman blames his tools

This old saying was definitely talking about a person with a fixed mindset.

Praise

Needing external validation in your life can be reinforced by the type of praise you were given as a child, or the type of praise you receive as an adult. When you are praised for your ability, being told you are smart and talented when you succeed, you are pushed into the fixed mindset.

Being praised for your ability has a negative flipside. If you succeeded because you have natural ability, what happens in the future if you encounter something you can't do? Does that mean you don't have any natural ability? Because the fixed mindset sees success as resulting from predetermined natural ability, failure must mean you don't have any. If you aren't smart today, then you were never smart, and can't become smarter in the future.

Parents and teachers often praise ability, because they think it will give a child greater sense of self worth and confidence. Although it comes from the purest of intentions, this type of positive reinforcement can make children afraid to make decisions. They worry more about not failing than learning. Praising ability undermines confidence rather than helping you feel better about yourself.

The thought that praise might cause a problem for those receiving it was first introduced to me in an article written by Carol Dweck. She shocked the world by publishing 'Caution – Praise Can be Dangerous.' Up until then, I believed that sincere praise was always a good thing to offer.

Dweck suggests that rather than praising someone's ability, you should praise their effort, how far they have progressed, and the learning strategies they have developed. When you focus on learning rather than natural talent, the growth mindset is being addressed.

In a study involving hundreds of adolescents, students were given ten challenging problems from a nonverbal IQ test. All the students achieved similar levels of success, were given their marks and assured that they had achieved a good score. The students were randomly divided into two groups. Half of the adolescents were praised for being smart, while the other half were praised for the effort they put in to getting their mark. When offered challenging new tasks to do that would help them develop other skills, a marked difference appeared between the two groups. Those who had been praised for their ability rejected trying the new tasks, while those who had been praised for effort welcomed the challenge.

Praising ability reinforces a fixed mindset, and can make people afraid to take risks in case they result in failure. You don't want to try something new in case you need to work hard to master it. Exerting effort doesn't fit with the picture of intelligence and natural ability that is held by those with the fixed mindset.

Praising effort and improvement reinforces a growth mindset. This is the best mindset to have if you want to be happy. It appreciates effort; there is no pressure to get it right the first time. How well you do doesn't reflect on the type of person you are. You are not defined by your accomplishments.

Making decisions that are not dependent on getting praise from others will teach you to look to yourself for validation. After all, you are the person who must live with the decision, so make one that feels good to you. Too few people have this skill. If friends and family begin to judge a decision you've made, do you have the strength to fall back on self-validation, or do you need their approval to be happy? I view this need for external approval to be one of the biggest hurdles when it comes to feeling happy.

Trusting Your Gut

I'm sure you have all made decisions based on a gut feeling. You can't quite put your finger on why you feel something is the correct thing to do, but you innately know it is. In school, teachers often tell their students to go with their first instinct when they are answering multiple choice questions and aren't sure of the answer. This isn't just an old wives' tale; this strategy has scientific backing.

The brain takes in far more information than it can possibly be aware of. Although it absorbs approximately 40,000 bits of information every second, it can only processes about 400 of those bits. That means much of the information your brain receives never reaches your consciousness.

Sitting through lectures may provide you with more knowledge than you realize. That's why going with your first instinct in a multiple-choice exam works. Your brain may know the answers to more questions that your mind realizes.

A word of caution: Don't think that you can have a gut instinct about what the winning lottery numbers are going to be. Winning the lottery involves luck rather than skill or understanding.

Being Lucky

There are people who classify themselves as naturally lucky, and others who believe the exact opposite applies. Google defines luck as 'success or failure brought by chance rather than through one's own actions.' If you win the lottery, that is a result of luck, not skill.

Richard Wiseman, a professor of psychology in England, became intrigued by the concept of luck, and researched the difference between people who thought they were lucky, and those who thought they were unlucky.

In one study, he chose a man who considered himself to be lucky and a woman who considered herself unlucky. Both were invited to a coffee shop for a meeting. They were instructed to go to a specific café, get themselves a drink, and then wait until a member of the production crew arrived.

For each meeting, the subjects were given two opportunities for something they might perceive as lucky to happen. A five-pound note was put on the ground directly outside the coffee shop, and inside the only place left for the person to sit was at a table with a successful businessman.

The lucky person picked up the money, entered the coffee shop, bought himself a drink and sat down with the businessman. He struck up a conversation that resulted in a business opportunity. The unlucky person stepped over the money, sat down at the table with the businessman, but didn't strike up a conversation, so didn't hear about the business opportunity.

Using this and many other studies, Richard Wiseman concluded that you make your own luck, and that you can learn to be luckier. The reason I mention this research within the chapter on making decisions is because of one of the four principles of luck that he established. Lucky people:

1. Are skilled at creating and noticing chance opportunities

2. Make lucky decisions by listening to their intuition

3. Create self-fulfilling prophesies via positive expectations

4. Adopt a resilient attitude that transforms bad luck into good

Listening to your intuition is the same as trusting your gut feelings. Remember, your brain has absorbed more information that you can possibly be conscious of. Trust that knowledge, and let your brain help you make good choices.

Helping with Decisions & Self-validation

Children tend to be encouraged to seek validation from others rather than from themselves. When they do something that their parents or teachers approve of, they are praised. If children aren't encouraged to make decisions that they believe are right, regardless of what anyone else thinks, they may end up relying on other people's opinions for their entire lives. This isn't a good situation for anyone who wants to create a life they are happy with.

You may grow up wanting to please the important people in your life, and make your decisions based on their reactions rather than how you feel about it. Have you ever done something that you really didn't want to do, just to see the smile on your partner's face?

There is nothing wrong with doing good things for others that don't benefit you, but your motivation needs to come from *your own* choice to do something for them, not because they think you should do it.

Letting Your Children Make Decisions

Every skill you possess has improved with practise. The earlier you start making decisions for yourself, the better you will become at it. There is nothing harder than standing back and letting your child risk failure – especially if you are a fixed mindset parent who worries that your child is going to be negatively affected if he doesn't succeed at everything he tries to achieve.

For many parents, letting go enough to allow your children to make decisions for themselves isn't easy. There are a couple of reasons for this. It is likely that your children have different personalities and characteristics from you. It's hard to accept that their path isn't yours, and what is right for you might not be right for them. The decisions they make may be different from the ones you would make in their place.

Sometimes you may think that parenting involves protecting your children from situations that are negative. Unless you adopt a growth mindset, and understand how important it is for your offspring to practise making choices and taking responsibility for their decisions, you aren't doing them any favors.

Dweck carried out a study on students who were transitioning to middle school. This can be a particularly difficult time for many as the work gets harder, there is less of a personal connection between students and teachers, and there are physical and hormonal changes taking place.

The research looked at students over a two-year period. The middle school had many new opportunities on offer, but those with a fixed mindset were afraid to try them in case they failed. They didn't want others to see them exerting effort to succeed, and they certainly didn't want to admit they were struggling and ask for help. This attitude is a detriment to learning, and the children in this group tended to do less well in their middle school grades than they had in elementary school.

On the other hand, the growth mindset students seemed to thrive in their new environment, and tended to get better grades. They didn't have a fear of failure, and took advantage of many of the new opportunities that were on offer. If they didn't understand something, they would ask for help, and then keep trying until they got it right. They didn't enter middle school believing that they should already know everything; they were there to learn.

Another difficult transition in education is the move from high school to university or college. It is much more difficult to earn top marks in post-secondary education, and yet a vast number of students working on their degrees are accustomed to achieving straight A's. Going from being a big fish in a small pond, to a small fish in a big pond full of top grade fish, can cause crisis for many fixed mindset scholars. Once again, research shows that those with a growth mindset will make this shift much more easily.

The Principle

Living a full, happy life includes making decisions and taking responsibility for their outcomes. The success or failure of your choices does not define who you are as a person. Help yourself with this concept by developing a growth mindset.

Life is full of opportunities to make decisions, although this is easier to do for some than it is for others. As a parent, you may feel you are more able to make good decisions for your children than they are for themselves, but if you don't help them learn decision making skills and the importance of taking responsibility, you are actually doing them a disservice. Remember, it is easier to make decisions if you have a growth mindset.

Gather information from others when you have a difficult decision to make, but ensure that the final choice is yours. Don't rely on the opinions of others to validate the conclusion you came to, or make a choice based purely on what they think. Learn to validate yourself; be strong in the conviction that you made the decision you thought was the right one.

Take responsibility for your decisions. When they don't work out as well as you had hoped, own the outcome and look for a lesson that can be learned, or an unexpected benefit. Use this information to help you the next time you have a decision to make.

Action

1. Practice making decisions

   Anyone who wants to be in control of the life they live needs to be willing to make decisions. Practice makes perfect, and although early decision making practice may feel uncomfortable, or even terrifying, the more you do it, the more you will become accustomed to it.

2. Model good decision making skills

   This is important if you want to help others learn to evaluate information and make choices that are right for them. Children learn many things from the adults that influence them. The best thing you can do to help your students and children learn to make decisions is to share with them decisions that you make, especially the ones that don't work out as expected.

   Share the process you took when you had to make a difficult choice, and tell them how you felt when others disagreed with your decision. Talking about what you learned is a reassuring way to let others see that making a mistake isn't as scary as they might think, and that sometimes the best things come from the worst failures.

When your four year-old doesn't want to wear a coat and you think they should, talk to them about the chance that they may get cold in a few minutes. If they remain adamant, set off without the coat. It is important that you don't slip it into your bag, or carry it for them if you want them to take responsibility for their decision.

CAUTION: You would never do this if the temperatures were below freezing, or if they were to complain of being cold fifteen minutes into a two-hour excursion. If you can't ensure a return home within a reasonable time, their choice might need to change. Informing them that they can't ski if they don't wear their jacket is another way to allow them to be in charge of a decision.

Is this easy to accomplish? No. In fact, teaching your children life skills is often harder than just taking the easy way. Listening to them complain that they're cold is more wearing than simply carrying their jacket until they decide they want it, but the easy way often isn't the best way to prepare them to be a well-adjusted, happy adult.

3. Don't provide a safety net

    As hard as it is, and I know this from experience, it is important that you don't provide a safety net that keeps your child from falling to the ground. If you do, your child will continue to believe that, regardless of what they do, you will always be there to save them. This doesn't teach autonomy skills. It can be hard to let go and watch your children become more independent and make mistakes, but it is important for you to do it.

4. Increase the number and type of decisions your students and children make as they mature

As your students and children mature and become successful at making decisions for themselves, give them more opportunities to be autonomous. There are numerous ways of doing this, so be creative depending on the personality and needs of your classroom or family. Give them other viewpoints to consider and suggestions that they may not have thought about, but remember the decision is theirs. They are the ones who must live with the outcome. If you take on ownership of the choice, you will also take on the blame if it doesn't work out as intended.

My best friend from high school and I both worked in our parents' campgrounds in the summer. At the end of the season, my friend was given $2,000 as her wages. That was all the money she would get until the next summer and she was responsible for buying all her own clothes, shampoo, etc.

In my family, I wasn't given any money. If I needed something, I would ask my parents for it. They paid for my clothes and personal needs, although I did get an allowance to cover small expenditures. I'm sure my parents spent an equal amount on me as my friend's parents did on her, if not more, but they had control over what was purchased.

I was happy with the arrangement, but remember, I was a fixed mindset girl in a house full of fixed mindset people. I didn't want to have to make decisions that might result in mistakes. My friend, on the other hand, was left to figure it out herself. If she made a mistake and ran out of money, she would learn to budget better. Her family didn't come rushing to the rescue.

Which approach was a better preparation for adulthood and perceiving personal influence?

5. Sleep on it

    When a difficult or unclear decision needs to be made, I council myself and others to sleep on it. After thinking about all the options and still being unsure of which direction to take, rest seems to clarify my thoughts. Often, I wake up with a feeling that tells me which decision is the right one. It wasn't until I started researching this book that I found out why this is.

    There are many studies that look at the effect of sleeping before making a big decision. Some suggest that only using your conscious mind to evaluate facts and come to a decision means that you may feel more certain that your decision is right, even if it isn't the best one.

    When you need to make an important decision, get your subconscious mind involved. In a study published in the Journal of Consumer Psychology, researchers asked participants to choose between a selection of cars. They were given information about safety ratings, gas mileage and extra features like cup holders and sunroofs.

    Some of the subjects were given time to sleep on the information before deciding and others were asked to make an immediate decision. The researchers wanted to see how many people chose a quality car over one with all the bells and whistles that got poor gas mileage and a poor safety rating. 90% of those who slept on their decision chose a quality car, while only 75% of the participants asked to decide immediately made the same choice.

Your subconscious mind is like a huge memory bank with virtually unlimited storage. It would be impossible for your brain to process all this information, so whatever it can't manage to pass onto your consciousness, it puts into your subconscious storage bank. This is where it sits until it is needed.

6. Use praise that works

    Instead of praising ability and intelligence, find ways to compliment progress, learning, and effort. Don't let words of admiration push its recipient into a fixed mindset, therefore making it more difficult for them to be robustly happy. Use praise that reinforces a growth mindset, to boost the happiness of the receiver.

Conclusion

When you are young you need to be guided on how to make decisions, but having the opportunity to make choices and live with the consequences is vital. This is how you learn to take responsibility for your life. For parents, watching your children fail can be excruciatingly painful, but remember you are there to guide, not to control. Letting them stumble and learn to recover is one of the greatest gifts you can give your students and children.

I know from personal experience how difficult this is, but taking the first fall at five is better than at twenty-five when the stakes are probably higher and the ground is much further away. As I endeavoured to make sure my son was getting his high school assignments handed in on time, my brother used to say this to me. It's better for him to fail a grade 10 course than one that is vital for his university degree. That is so true, but so hard to stand by and watch. Sometimes we need to let others fail before they are ready to achieve the next level on their journey. It could be that when things seem to be falling apart, the pieces are simply falling into place.

Turn to yourself for validation, rather than to those around you. Only you can understand the journey you are taking, so ultimately only you can appreciate the big picture. Help your students and children to consider the opinions of others, but to trust their ability to make choices for themselves. No one else lives your life, so ensure it is the right one for you.

Throughout this book, I am encouraging you to decide to be happy. You may be living a very happy life, but if you haven't chosen for it to be that way, you may be living with a very fragile type of happiness. Will a bump in the road cause that delicate well-being to shatter? That is what happened to me when I went from my happy life in Canada to a challenging life in Britain. I hadn't made the choice to be happy, so I had no idea how to re-establish it when it disappeared from my life.

Trust yourself to make decisions and then take responsibility for them, knowing that it seemed like the best choice at the time. If making decisions is difficult for you, understand that not making decisions is also a choice. It's your life, so you might as well be the one responsible for it.

Precept 4 – Change Your Perspective

Although you may think you see with your eyes, it is probably more accurate to say you see with your brain. Your optic nerve sends information from your retina to your brain, where the images are interpreted.

Optical Illusions

I remember a day in junior high when we were shown a picture that contained both the face of a young woman and the face of an old lady. To start with, I could only see the older one and was sure that was all there was, but with a little help from my teacher, the second face came into focus.

Perhaps you have seen this picture, or one like it. There is another famous one that contains both a candle stick and two faces in profile. You tend to see one image immediately, and have to look a little harder to see the second one.

These optical illusion picture duos clearly mimic life. At first glance you may interpret what you see in a particular way, but with enough time and consideration, another way of translating the event may become evident. Is the glass half full, or half empty? If it has exactly 50% of its volume filled with water, then the glass is both half full and half empty. The same image information is sent to your brain, regardless of which viewpoint you choose to believe. Ultimately, the interpretation of the amount of water in the glass comes from your brain.

You decide whether to see it half full, or half empty.

Optimist or Pessimist?

Is it failure, or an opportunity to learn?
Are you a cashier, or a customer service professional?
Is your glass half full, or half empty?

All three of these questions have more than one answer. Understanding you have a choice when it comes to interpreting your life is important if you want to be happy.

Sophie Chou, a psychology researcher at National Taiwan University, has discovered that realistic optimists are more likely to be happy and successful than either pessimists or people who are unrealistically optimistic. The Mail Online defines a realistic optimist as 'someone who looks on the bright side of life, but has a realistic grasp on the present, and what to expect in life.'

Many pessimists tell me that they aren't negative, they are just being realistic. This is true, but the optimist is also being realistic. How can both viewpoints think they are representing a truer reflection of life than the other? Remember that only an approximate 400 of the 40,000 bits of information your brain takes in get processed. How does it know what to process and what to store?

Your brain is programed to support your thoughts and beliefs, so if you think something won't work out, chances are it won't. On the other hand, if you believe it will work out, then your brain will process information that supports that viewpoint. Your brain works tirelessly to support your beliefs, which is one of the reasons why two people in the same situation may perceive it differently. Changing your perspective can help your viewpoint become a more positive one.

Janitor or Caring Professional?

Psychologist Amy Wrzesniewski decided to look at how people in unglamorous jobs coped with work that tended to be seen as undesirable.

The study focused on interviewing cleaning staff at large hospitals in Midwest America. The results were largely consistent with the expectations of the research team - in all hospitals but one. In this facility, the janitors didn't see themselves as being part of the cleaning staff; instead they saw themselves as caring professionals. The perceived the work they did as more than just cleaning; they supported visiting families in a multitude of small, yet valuable ways. They produced Kleenex and water when needed, made a connection with the families, and were there to listen. One worker reported changing the pictures in the rooms of comatose patients in the hope that a change of scenery would help them recover.

These people were still cleaning the floors and bathrooms, and doing all the other chores assigned to the janitorial staff, but they had changed the perspective they used to view the work they did. They believed their job was making a positive difference in the lives of others, rather than seeing it as a mundane, undervalued position.

Choosing a Lucky Perspective

Think back to the study Richard Wiseman set up for the lucky man and the unlucky lady. Both these people had the same opportunities, yet only one person took advantage of them. Believing that she was unlucky meant the woman viewed life through a lens that took more notice of things she could interpret as unlucky. The man, on the other hand, believed he was lucky, and because of that faith, he was.

Further research by Wiseman revealed that people who believe they are lucky are constantly scanning their environment for opportunity. They are more likely to strike up conversations with random people. You never know who might cross your path, or what might happen as a result.

The Principle

Many of the things that affect you in life are beyond your control. You can't choose whether they happen, but you can choose how you react to them. You can look for hidden benefits that accompany challenges, or you can complain and seek a scape-goat to blame. Hidden blessings don't always reveal themselves immediately, but when you look back on difficult times, you may notice that as a result of it you learned a new skill, stepped out of your comfort zone, or developed an inner strength you didn't have before.

Change your perspective when you feel badly treated by others. Try giving them the benefit of the doubt rather than flaring up and expending a lot of energy in a negative reaction. You don't know what is happening in someone else's life; they may be reacting to a circumstance they can't control, and you are receiving their frustration. Taking a more even-tempered approach, and giving others the benefit of the doubt, will transform your life.

How you view the events that happen to you is a matter of choice. Preventing a negative cloud from descending takes practice, but is worth the effort if you want to model robust happiness.

Action

1. Be a role model

    Actively share with others how you are looking at situations from different perspectives. If someone cuts you off when you are driving, talk about why that person might have chosen to do it. Trying to see it from the other driver's viewpoint can make it easier to accept their actions without becoming annoyed.

2. Look at optical illusions

    Study how the same image can be seen in more than one way.

3. Show pictures of signs like pedestrian crossing

    What else could this sign mean? Encourage creativity.

4. Make and/or look through a kaleidoscope

    Discuss how the same pieces can be combined in many ways to make different patterns. It's a new way of looking at the same objects.

5. Create Tangrams

    Use puzzles where the pieces can be arranged in a variety of ways to make different shapes.

6. Practice viewing events from different perspectives

    Use story characters and events, or real life situations. Brainstorm unseen benefits in challenges that are being faced. Take an unpleasant interaction, and see if you can look at it from a different perspective.

7. Find the humor in negative situations

I discovered the best way to deal with embarrassing events was to remind myself they would make the best funny stories the next time I wanted to entertain my family or friends.

8. Watch or read *Pollyanna* and try playing the Glad Game

Although the main character in this story is sickly sweet, she is on the right track when it comes to viewing events through a new lens in an effort to be happy.

9. Give others the benefit of the doubt

When your first reaction is to think the worst of other people, try to view an unpleasant situation from another perspective.

10. Look for the lessons in challenging experiences

Can you learn anything from a negative experience? What positive nugget can you take away?

Conclusion

How you view what happens to you in life is a choice. Remember that you can't control external circumstances, but you can control how you react to them. Follow the Pollyanna Principle and look for something positive in what has happened, or find a lesson you've learned from the challenges you face.

Choose to give people the benefit of the doubt rather than thinking the worst of them; look for good things that may arise from the challenges you face or failures you encounter. These decisions will go a long way toward creating a life that contains more positive than negative. You may not recognize the benefits of undesirable experiences immediately; it can take time and refection to recognize the lesson in a seemingly negative event. Don't rush the process. Learn to trust that something useful is likely to reveal itself at some point.

Help yourself and others change how they view themselves and their environment. Model this attitude, even if you struggle with your negative inner voice. I chose not to 'diet' when my daughter was growing up. Instead I modified my diet to be healthier when I felt the need arise. I didn't want her to think it was normal behavior for women to starve themselves so they could be thinner. It was a good exercise for me, but I had to battle my inner demons the entire time.

Some of the most cheerful, positive people I have ever met have been individuals struck by circumstances that many people would buckle under. A young boy with brittle bones comes to mind when I think of these situations. He was a positive, caring, optimistic child, even though he lived with an incredibly serious health condition. He didn't bemoan his situation, he embraced it and lived his life to the fullest he could.

There is always more than one way to view any situation, and a lesson to be learned when times are tough. Choosing the lens of positivity will help create a life of robust happiness.

Precept 5 – Be Curious

Swiss psychologist Dr. Jean Piaget defined curiosity as the urge to explain the unexpected. I like to define it as the need to learn more about yourself and the world around you. You are born with a natural inquisitiveness that helps you learn and develop. Sadly, many people lose this natural curiosity as they age, and with it goes their drive to be a life-long learner.

What stops our natural curiosity? Research links the awareness of others evaluating us with the decline of inquisitiveness. So many children enter school as curious sponges, ready to absorb new information, only to discover the existence of the grading system. Discovering the number of ways you can find to make noises with your chair doesn't seem to rate highly on report cards. It becomes more important to achieve the goals the teacher sets out than it does to learn.

The Problem with Comparison

I've already shared how terrible I was at team sports when I was in school. The only thing that ever gave me some relief from my feelings of failure in this field was when a student joined the school who was equally as bad as me or, if I was lucky, even worse. It didn't happen often, but when it did, it made me happy. Knowing that there was someone with even worse skills gave me comfort. I might be a failure, but there were people in the world who were bigger failures than me.

For the most part, comparing yourself to others is a

negative activity. By comparing, you are looking for validation that you are doing all right, or at the very least that you are doing better than someone else.

The fixed mindset is much more concerned with comparison as a way to protect their own image. If you have a growth mindset, you are less concerned about how you stack up against others, and more interested in your own journey of learning.

When you play the comparison game, your observations of others may not be an accurate reflection of what is really going on with them. From your perspective, it may look like everything is wonderful, but that may not always be the case.

Think about the saying 'The grass is always greener on the other side.' It rarely is, but from where you are standing you can't see all the crab grass, weeds and sparse patches that are clearly visible when you look at your own lawn. If you climbed over the fence and stood in the other person's grass, it may not look any different from your own.

Comparing yourself to someone who seems to be doing better can be a very destructive activity. Remind yourself that you can't really know what is going on in someone else's life unless you are living it.

Competition or Collaboration?

The mindset you adopt has a lot to do with how successful you are at collaboration. This is an important skill to possess when you are part of a team. Putting the success of the group, or family, ahead of your own individual achievements is necessary if you want to create a cohesive unit. Constantly comparing yourself to others and trying to make sure you are the winner is a disaster when it comes to working cooperatively.

The fixed mindset looks for comfort in finding someone with grass that is worse than their own, constantly checking to see how they stack up against the accomplishments of others. They see life as a series of competitions where only one person can win, so being part of a team can prove challenging and frustrating. What if the others don't want to use your ideas? How can you appear all-knowing if someone else's ideas are considered to be better than yours?

Unless everything you do within the group can be accomplished with the appearance of effortless brilliance, the person with the fixed mindset may well prefer to do nothing at all. When times get tough, the fixed mindset tends to give up. This can cause animosity in teamwork situations, rather than creating a group of cohesive individuals that are working together towards success.

With a growth mindset, you are better prepared to be part of a team. You tend to seek win-win scenarios, and are less concerned about comparing yourself to others. A win for the team is a win for you. This makes collaborative work easier to participate in successfully.

Curiosity and the Aging Brain

Not that many decades ago, it was believed that brains developed and grew until a certain age, and then the brain cells slowly started to die off. You expected that as you aged, you would become less able to learn new things, find your existing skills diminishing and your brain working less efficiently. New research has discovered that this is not the case at all.

Scientists are learning that the human brain has a much greater capacity for learning and development than anyone ever thought possible. The study of neuroplasticity shows that the pathways in our brains can develop and strengthen, even as we age. Your brain is like a muscle; the more you use it, the stronger it gets; the less you use it, the weaker it gets.

Constantly improving your skills, regardless of how advanced they already are, is the behavior of a life-long learner. Why do professional athletes continue to get coaching, even though they may already be ranked number one in the world? They are striving to continue improving, even if it is by the smallest of margins. Setting goals and working to achieve them is one of the needed nine elements of happiness, as well as an intentional activity referred to in the Happiness Equation.

Curiosity and School

I did well in my post-secondary courses. I learned how to listen to the professor and parrot back their values and viewpoints. This resulted in good grades, but not necessarily in becoming more knowledgeable or more skilful. The school system would be so much better if we could encourage more love of learning, and less reward for getting the right answer.

Every year curious children start school, only to discover the world of letter grades. When they are rewarded with an A, parents and teachers smile, say well done and shine the spotlight on them. This is especially true if you are working with fixed mindset teachers or parents.

Suddenly your curiosity for learning has competition. Many children stop learning because they are curious, and instead start focusing on getting a good letter grade. Their motivation changes completely; they want validation from the adults in their lives. They would rather complete activities they know they can do and which will result in a good grade, instead of nourishing their curiosity and choosing a more challenging path that will help them learn more.

The curious mind has a much better chance of surviving the school years intact if its owner has a growth mindset, as these minds value learning over the need to get good grades and receive external validation.

Individual Learning Rates

At birth, your brain is only partially developed. Knowing as we do that brains change every time they learn something or practice a skill, it shouldn't surprise you to discover that brains develop at their own pace. If you look at ten twelve-year-olds, you will see a huge range in height, weight, and physical development. We accept that without much thought, but would it surprise you to discover that there is just as much variation in the development of their brains?

Everything you learn and do creates physical changes in your brain. The pathways that are created or reinforced are different for each of us. We all experience life differently and thus the way our brain wires itself is unique. This is also true for identical twins, even if they are sharing the same experiences.

As parents and teachers, you need to bear this in mind when you are interacting with children. To expect that everyone of the same age will be ready to learn the same skills is like suggesting that everyone should reach puberty by the time they are twelve. It is unrealistic.

This is another reason the growth mindset makes learning more rewarding. Being slower to develop some skills doesn't label you as slow, nor does it suggest that you won't ever be as talented as your compatriots, who may have mastered the same skills at a younger age. Students need learning environments that respect individual differences and give more credit to effort than being an early learner. A child who is one of the youngest in his year, or grade, at school, can be at a huge disadvantage in the fixed mindset world.

How Curiosity Increases Happiness

Having an opportunity to use your abilities is one of the features that creates feelings of positivity about school and work.

This feature addresses two sides of your abilities: the skills you already possess, and the opportunity to gain new ones. It is part of human nature to enjoy doing things that you are good at. Most people find it enjoyable to participate in activities where they already feel comfortable and somewhat competent.

I was never very good at sports, but instead of practicing shooting a basketball I would spend my time reading or creating music. Those were things I was good at and enjoyed, so they were the abilities I invested myself in. Perhaps I should have been improving my basketball skills, but that doesn't fit with human nature. The kids who spend all their time shooting hoops are more likely to be the ones who are already reasonably good at it, or at least *see* themselves as being good at it. Remember, perception is key.

Because we feel happier when we are doing things we believe we are proficient at, being given the opportunity to use these abilities will give you a huge boost of satisfaction.

Attaining new skills is also important if you want to increase your happiness. Research consistently shows that people who continue to learn new skills have a greater level of satisfaction. It is also increases confidence and self-validation.

The actual process of learning a new skill may not be a

painless one, however. Ryan Howell, an assistant professor at San Francisco State University, calls it the 'No Pain No Gain' rule. Although the initial process of learning something new may cause you to feel stressed while you are doing it, you will feel happy and satisfied when you look back after having become successful at it. Keep this in mind the next time you want to quit before you master a new competency. You need to suffer through the pain to gain the happiness.

Remember that your brain is creating and strengthening neural pathways whenever you work on new skills. Rather than giving up, picture what is happening in your head and rest assured that the struggle will be worth the effort.

The Principle

Happy people are life-long learners. Constantly finding opportunities to learn new things comes from a sense of curiosity. You were born with a very inquisitive nature, but unless you were encouraged to nurture it, it may well have disappeared, at least to some degree.

Rediscover your spirit of curiosity by honoring effort and improvement, rather than effortless natural ability. Model a mind that is interested in new experiences, knowledge, and understanding. See wonder in the world around you, and strive to learn more about yourself and your environment. Modelling an inquisitive nature will encourage you to look for learning opportunities throughout your entire life.

Action

1. Be a role model

Encourage your curiosity and make a commitment to learn new skills. If youngsters see adults continuing to ask questions about the world they live in, in order to learn more, they will be more likely to adopt these same attitudes as they grow into adulthood. Model your choice to be a life-long learner.

2. Brain Work

Teach students about the brain and what happens to it when they learn.

Use rope, string, thread, and other materials to demonstrate how neural pathways are created and strengthened as you learn new skills.

3. Honor Effort

Praise effort rather than ability. Help students imagine what is happening in their brains when they are exerting effort or learning new skills.

Journal each day and ask students to record what they learned and what they had to work hard at.

Ask your children what they learned at school that day and what took effort for them to achieve. This is a great supper time activity, or a conversation to have on the way home from school if you are picking them up. Don't accept that they didn't learn anything, and if they said they didn't have to try to achieve anything, help them understand that they weren't strengthening their brains if they didn't have to work hard. Praise them for effort exerted rather than ability possessed.

4. Move Out of Your Comfort Zone

Provide opportunities and support that allow students to take a small step out of their comfort zone.

- Try a new game or sport
- Taste different types of food
- Share times when you stepped out of your comfort zone and lived to tell the tale
- Ask students who enjoy leaving their comfort zones to share their experiences and strategies
- Look for story characters who are out of their comfort zone. Discuss/write about what this person felt during and after the experience
- If appropriate, try a trust walk or trust fall activity
- Celebrate students who have tried something new or nerve-wracking

Conclusion

There is no reason for your curiosity to die as you grow older, but it does. We stop learning or striving for new goals, choosing instead to rest on our laurels and enjoy what we have already achieved.

To model happiness, it is vital that you rediscover your inquisitive nature. This will become easier if you ensure you are viewing the world with a growth mindset. Try something new without the fear of failure, set goals that are just out of your reach and then create a strategy to attain them, or take a few steps out of your comfort zone. As professional speaker Linda Edgecombe loves to say, 'When was the last time you did something for the first time?'

Precept 6 – Connect with Others

At the end of a long summer away from school, I asked my son if he was looking forward to getting back to class. He thought for a few moments before telling me he was excited to see all his classmates, but he really didn't want to go back to school.

This is not an unusual sentiment, and isn't limited to students. Have you ever had a job that you didn't really like, but you stayed with because you liked your colleagues, and felt like you were part of the team?

Dr. Brene Brown, a research professor at the University of Houston Graduate College of Social Work writes, 'A deep sense of love and belonging is an irresistible need of all people. We are biologically, cognitively, physically, and spiritually wired to love, to be loved, and to belong. When those needs are not met, we don't function as we were meant to. We break. We fall apart. We numb. We ache. We hurt others. We get sick.'

It is important to recognize that feeling connected has nothing to do with the number of connections you have. More is not necessarily better. The key is to *perceive* that you have a link with another person. As with so many other topics you have read in this book, the key to success is *believing* you are connected, not in persuading others to think you are. If you feel attached to another person, it doesn't matter whether they view your friendship the same way or not. You will benefit from being connected.

Social Connection and Personality Types

There is variation in the amount and type of social contact different personality types need, but it is essential for everyone to have some level of social connection if they want to live a life of robust happiness.

There is a mistaken belief that introverts prefer to be on their own. This may be true to some extent, but even people who love their own company are hardwired to seek out the companionship of others. They may prefer to be around only a few people at a time, or avoid situations where they are expected to make small talk for extended periods, but everyone needs connections with others.

I love my own company and believed I was an introvert until I became Myers Briggs certified when I was in my early 50s. It turns out I am an extravert who changed schools a lot. With my fixed mindset that *knew* I wasn't very smart, I lacked the self-confidence necessary to put myself out there and risk rejection. How did I manage to feel connected when I moved schools so often and was timid when it came to making social links?

As a child, I was very connected with my family and I always made a few close friends each time I moved. As I entered adulthood, I still made sure I had family and close friends in my life, but I also got in the habit of striking up conversations with cashiers, other people waiting in lines, and random people whose paths crossed mine. I perceived a connection with each of these interactions. It didn't matter how the other person felt; I received a little jolt of positivity each time I created a short-lived connection. My perception of the interaction ensured that I felt connected.

The amount and type of social contact you desire is very individual. Some of you crave constant company, while others prefer to spend more time alone or interacting one-on-one. Some of you do your best work while being surrounded by the energy of other people. For others, hearing constant conversations means you are unable to get your work done. Regardless of where you fit in the scheme of social contact, you all need some interaction to be happy.

If you don't spend enough time with others, you may become lonely. If you spend too much time with them, you may become frustrated. Neither of these states is desirable. It is also important to consider the type of contact you are having. Negative interactions aren't going to foster a feeling of well-being. For some people, their greatest source of unhappiness is the people they network with.

Connecting in the World of Technology

No discussion on social connection and youth would be complete without addressing the role and impact of technology. There is no doubt that the way we interact has changed, but if we are going to be true to our species, we need to change along with our environment. I don't believe that cell phones and computers are going to disappear, so you need to find ways to work with them to nurture social connection.

Nothing can take the place of face-to-face interaction, but technology can be an aid to strengthening it. Have you ever watched a group of work mates bond in the lunch room by discussing a popular book, movie, or mini series? I've made amazing connections with other ladies who are Costco groupies. Shared experiences are incredibly powerful glue; you don't have to watch the program together to bond by discussing it. Playing online games with other people, especially if you have a face-to-face relationship with them as well, is still a type of social interaction. You are sharing an experience and communicating, even if you can't see them.

I feel much more connected with family and friends that don't live near me, because I keep in contact through Facebook. I have also made friends with people online before meeting them in person. When I met them for the first time, I already felt like I knew them. The online experience had created a connection that was then strengthened face-to-face.

Technology isn't necessarily a bad thing. It can help nurture relationships. The problem comes if you allow it to replace traditional relationships. As a role model, you can develop and demonstrate ways to use technology as a supplemental way to foster and strengthen friendships or business associations.

Researchers from the University of Florida surveyed 339 students to discover if using smart phones reduced their social capital. This expression is defined by Dictionary.com as 'the network of social connections that exist between people, which enable and encourage mutually advantageous social cooperation.' Even though participants reportedly spent 100-200 minutes a day on the internet and 30-90 minutes daily on social media, every one of them had a positive amount of social capital and weren't at all socially isolated.

At the other end of the age spectrum, studies looked at whether social media sites help seniors stay connected. Findings show that the participants benefited from better health, less chance of reduced cognitive skills, and longer lives if they used sites like Facebook. Only a small percentage of American adults over the age of 65 use Facebook. This may be in part because of the age they were at when social media became popular. Perhaps we should be encouraging seniors to start using social media now. It is never too late to learn a new skill.

The Happy Chicken & Socially Connected Egg

In the section on the Importance of Emotions, I shared with you how people who feel mildly to moderately happy find it is easier to make new friends. When you have friends, it is easier to feel happy, and if you are happy, you are more likely to make new friends.

Do you need social connections to feel happy, or do you need to feel happy first so you can make social connections? These elements are so closely linked that it is difficult to separate them, making it a chicken-and-egg type situation. Although you could debate which one came first, I don't think it really matters. The important thing is to understand that social connection is vital if you want to be happy.

One company I worked for provided Friday lunches if we made sales targets for the previous month. It was a great incentive, enjoyed by everyone. We didn't get much of a chance to gather together as a group during the work day, so these lunches helped us bond.

One year, we missed the targets for February and because the shortfall was added to what needed to be achieved for the next month's target, there were no more Friday lunches – for the rest of the year.

The change in moral and team spirit was overwhelming. Taking away the opportunity to strengthen our social connection did untold damage to the strength of the company.

The Principle

Humans are social creatures with a basic need to spend time with others and to be accepted by them. It renews your sense of belonging and purpose. Connection is more than just being in the same space, it is about creating a link or relationship with another person. The more connected you feel, the happier you are. Having friends is a powerful force when it comes to happiness. You may be nervous about doing something by yourselves, but put a few friends by your side and chances are you will become a superhero.

Research shows there are many health benefits associated with being socially connected, including an increased immune system, lower levels of anxiety and depression, longer life-spans, and greater self-esteem. A landmark study by House, Landis and Umberson suggests that a lack of social connection negatively affects your health more than obesity, smoking and high blood pressure combined.

Action

1. Respect and honor your connections

    Model behavior that respects others and honors individual differences. This includes creating a non-judgemental attitude towards other people. Just because they do things differently to you doesn't mean their way isn't just as good as yours. If they aren't harming you or anyone else, there is no valid reason for you to stand in judgement.

2. Try to be a source of positive energy for the people you interact with

Emotions are contagious. If you enter a room of happy people, you are likely to find yourself feeling happy. The same goes if you surround yourself with negativity. If you make a concentrated effort to be a source of positive energy, the people who meet you will benefit from it.

3. Create safe environments and accepting cultures

    A safe environment where everyone is accepted will do wonders to put your students and children in the right mindset to learn. The negative emotions that arise from a hostile environment make learning almost impossible.

    Make sure your home and school environments honor individual differences and accept that each person is on their own journey of learning. You don't need to be friends with everyone you work or go to school with, but you do need to feel accepted and safe.

4. Create connections with the people in your life

    Spend energy getting to know the people you interact with. Find out a little bit about them, and let them get to know you, too. If you are a teacher, make a connection with every student you teach.

    This can be a challenge if you are a subject teacher rather than a classroom teacher, but with effort, it is doable. I'm not suggesting that you need to be their best friend, but talk to them enough that you know what they like, what their hobbies are, and maybe a little about their home-life. Let them get to know a little bit about you too.

5. Ensure your students have opportunities to work with

others in partner or group activities

Having an opportunity to get to know someone better can help create a positive - or at least more tolerant - connection between members of different social or personality groups. When group or partner work gets tough, remind students that they are building new and helpful neural pathways and learning skills that will serve them well when they get into the working world.

6. Choose to view others through a positive lens

Accept everyone even if they aren't people you would be best friends with. Look for ways to appreciate what they have to offer. When difficulties arise, look for win-win solutions, and remember to give them the benefit of the doubt.

7. Make family-time a tradition

Build family activity habits into your life. If everyone is accustomed to these events happening on a regular basis, you are less likely to stop connecting as a unit.

Conclusion

The importance of social connection in the classroom, staffroom and family unit cannot be underestimated. How happy you feel has a lot to do with your connections with others. Social connection was essential in order for humans in more primitive times to survive. Today, we are still wired to seek out relationships with others.

With suicide rates among youths accounting for almost

one in four deaths, more attention needs to be devoted to the importance of ensuring that children have opportunities to connect with other people, as this is an excellent way to create happy people, living happy lives.

Connecting at School

As a teacher of children between the ages of eight and fourteen, I rarely had any difficulties with discipline. This was largely because I made a connection with every child I taught. I talked to them when issues arose and helped them to choose to stay within the accepted boundaries of behavior in my classroom.

It wasn't until I substituted in a school I had never taught in before that I realized just how important that strategy was for me to be a happy teacher. I was in a grade eight class in a private school, and for the first time in my history as a teacher, I struggled to keep behavior within acceptable limits. I decided that substituting was not the job for me, although had I continued to go into the school and concentrated on making connections with the students, I am sure I would have overcome the problem.

Connecting at Home

How you connect with your family is a very individual decision. I am not suggesting that my family is another version of the Waltons, but we still love spending time together. Let me give you some ideas of ways you can connect with your loved ones, by sharing a few of the ways we stayed connected, even during the teenage years.

We created family traditions when our children were young.

On the weekends, we would find time to play board games together, go to playgrounds, and watch movies. Even though my husband frequently slept through the Disney favourites, we were all together in the same room, doing something as a family. My children are now in their early 20s and we still play board games and watch movies together. For some families, it is skiing or playing sports as a group. It doesn't matter what activity you choose as long as everyone is interacting and enjoying themselves. When it comes to board games, you may not feel like everyone is enjoying themselves when arguing, or tempers kick in, but helping your children learn to lose is a valuable skill. This is the perfect opportunity to reinforce a growth mindset.

We made the decision for our family not to have televisions in the bedrooms. I think of TV as a social activity, not as something to do by yourself. We watch, discuss, and sometimes argue while having a shared experience. When televisions are in bedrooms, the experience becomes very isolated and anti-social. Having televisions in shared areas means that you may watch programs you aren't really interested in, but knowing what your family is viewing and being able to join in conversations about favorite programs more than pays for it in my opinion.

The family rule is no cell phones or tablets at the table. If you get a message or call, you can wait until dinner is over to reply. I also use this rule when we are in the car together. When my daughter and I go shopping, I expect her to give her attention to me, not to her phone. If she has to respond to a message, she apologizes and keeps the time she uses for it to an absolute minimum. During family interaction times, the face-to-face relationships take priority.

Precept 7 - Take Action

Change only happens when you act. The importance of appreciating the distinction between having knowledge and putting strategies into action cannot be underestimated. Far too many people have a dream that never becomes reality because they are afraid to fail, or don't feel able to put their plan into action. The dream fades and becomes no more than a fantasy.

Taking even a small step towards a goal gives you the opportunity to make a dream come true. Many long journeys are made up of small steps. You don't have to travel the entire way in one fell swoop.

Choosing to act on the values and beliefs you hold is a vital part of transformation. The forces that you encounter in life are going to make a bigger impact on you if you are already in motion. Sitting at home by yourself, reading books about happiness, will not make you happier. You have to take the information you've learned, then go into the world and make it happen through your actions.

Tips to Help You Take Action

Plan

If you know the direction you want to travel in, it is much easier to take a path that will get you there. If you have no idea where you're headed, you are much more likely to wander aimlessly, or even just stand still. Decide what you want to achieve and come up with one or two things that will help you to bring it about.

'Just do it' is the tagline for Nike, but I think it should be a mantra for everyone. Getting started is just that: a beginning. You can modify your goal as you progress, if you decide it isn't quite right. Nothing is set in stone, and being adaptable is a skill that needs constant practice. Plan a route, and take your first step. You can adjust your course as you travel.

The One Percent Philosophy

Do you believe in the 'all or nothing' approach to life? I call this the 100% philosophy. It means that you either do things with total commitment, or not at all. Expecting to transform yourself into a happiness model within a short period may not be realistic, nor is it likely to occur without some bumps and dips in your journey.

With the 100% philosophy, you are likely to start your transformation with passion and determination. You may have initial success, but what happens when you hit it a bump in the road? You wake up one day to discover you just don't feel like being optimistic. You want to wallow in negativity and complain about your life.

This is when the 100% approach may let you down. Instead of your bad mood and lack of energy upsetting your efforts for one day, people with this philosophy often feel that by straying off the path, even just a tiny bit, it is no longer worth taking that route at all. One slip and all positivity and growth mindset strategies are quickly and completely forgotten. You return to your previous attitudes and behaviors.

These people have created such a high standard for

themselves that any weakness or detour means they have failed in their attempt to achieve that goal. Rather than seeing failure as an indication of something they need to continue to work on, they give up. If they can't do something unerringly, then they might as well not do it at all. Do you recognize the fixed mindset in this behavior?

I am not the type of person who sets the bar too high for myself, and for perhaps the first time in my life, I have found a reason why my 'good enough' approach might be better than the one held by my high-achieving, perfection-loving friends.

I'm not lazy, and I love to set and attain goals just as much as the next person, but I don't feel driven to be perfect. I am quite content to do what I can, and willingly accept that I will stumble from time to time. I don't lose a moment of sleep over it. Tomorrow is a new day and I am perfectly satisfied with taking small steps towards success.

I call this the 1% philosophy: from small changes come big differences. If you move forward, it doesn't matter how quickly or slowly you are going, just don't give up. In words from the Chinese classic text of Toa Te Ching,

The journey of a thousand miles begins with a single step.

The thought of dropping from a philosophy of 100% to 1% may horrify you, however I urge all of you one hundred percenters to join me. I like to think of the 1% approach as tweaking your life rather than changing it completely.

Do one little thing every day that will move you in the direction you want to go. Choose to give your friends the benefit of the doubt, add one intentional activity to your life, or decide to connect with one new person. Don't think every choice must be 100%; 1% is a viable, and sometimes preferable, option. Remember that one misstep only takes you a small way off your path; you can easily find your way back to the original trail.

The Serenity Prayer Philosophy

God grant me the serenity to accept the things I cannot change;

Courage to change the things I can

And wisdom to know the difference

I know I included this prayer earlier in the book, but its sentiment is important to remember when you are considering action. Worrying, fussing, and feeling frustrated about things you can't change is a waste of your time and energy. It is important to identify the things in your life that you have both the desire to change, and that *can* be changed. This takes conscious thought and reflection. The more you practice recognizing the difference between the things that can be altered and those that can't, the easier it becomes.

Some people like to bemoan what is happening in the world, but aren't prepared to do anything about it. I have chosen not to spend my mental energy worrying about things I'm not prepared to try and change. I'm concerned with how we treat the earth, so I recycle, pick up litter and try not to waste energy by leaving lights on. I choose to take small steps that will make a difference if we all do them.

On the other hand, I have no control over who will be the next president of the United States, so I choose not to waste my time discussing it endlessly. Unless I'm willing to stand up and act, I try not to spend my energy focusing on events and people that result in pessimistic thoughts.

The things you are willing to take action on will not be the same as everyone else around you. Choosing which battles are worth fighting is a very individual decision.

Be Wary of Unrealistic Expectations

How often do you find yourself disappointed in a movie that everyone else loved, or go to a party full of anticipation, only to find it wasn't as much fun as you had imagined? Modifying your expectations can increase your happiness.

I don't want anyone to think they can't aim high when they are setting goals; you should do exactly that, especially when it comes to your performance and accomplishments, but keep your expectations about how and when everything will fall into place realistic.

When I was on a commonwealth teaching exchange in my twenties, I decided I couldn't return home without a visit to Egypt. I didn't know anyone else who wanted to go, so I booked myself on to a tour. I didn't think being on my own would be a problem, because I assumed the tour would consist of a large bus full of English-speaking travellers. When I arrived in Cairo, I discovered that I was the only person on my tour. For some people that wouldn't have been a problem, but I was nervous about being in such a different culture all on my own. My expectations hadn't matched the reality I was given, and my first reaction was panic.

In actual fact, the time I spent in Egypt was a fabulous learning experience, and I discovered inner strength I never knew I had. Being disappointed isn't always a bad thing, but remember we are talking about happiness, and I'm pretty sure the happiest I was during that ten day Egyptian holiday was when I boarded the plane to return to England.

It is better to expect that the path you have chosen will

have bumps and dips in it, rather than convincing yourself it will be paved and easy to walk along. Being pleasantly surprised by how well maintained the route is will encourage you to continue, while being disappointed in how much worse it is than you had imagined may leave you disheartened.

The Endowed Progress Effect

The first steps toward any goal are often the most difficult. I believe that the first step is always the hardest, especially if it involves stepping out of your comfort zone.

This Endowed Progress Effect was researched by Nunes and Dreze and suggests that when people feel they have made progress towards a goal, they are more likely to become committed to reaching it.

Have you ever found yourself staying at work later than you had planned, just so you could finish a report? You would be less likely to put that extra time into the endeavour if you were just starting out with the project. The closer you are to reaching a goal, the harder you work to achieve it.

If you are like me, you may think it is best to get the worst stuff out of the way first, but if you make the initial steps of your goal as easy to achieve as possible, you can put the Endowed Progress Effect to work. Save the more difficult steps until the end, when you are invested in the project. This can help you with the push you need to get the harder things done, rather than just giving up on them.

When you find yourself struggling to see a project through to the end, stop and reflect on how far you have already come. That mental reminder might be just the incentive you need to stick it out.

Live in the Moment

When you are working toward a goal, it is easy to focus on it so hard that you forget about what's already happening in your life. The same can be said about your past. You may have suffered through ordeals that affected you so much that you have trouble moving on from them.

Being consciously mindful of what is happening in your life *now* has been shown to help people:

1. Deal with long term medical conditions

2. Have lower levels of the stress hormone cortisol

3. Achieve greater emotional stability

4. Experience a better quality of sleep

Your body lives in the present, but your mind very rarely does unless you make a conscious effort to put it there. Happiness needs to be experienced, so it goes hand in hand with living in the moment. Don't let yourself become one of those people who plan on being happy at some point in the future, such as when they retire or find a new job. Make sure you are happy in the here and now.

My husband and I recently decided to go to Costa Rica. We love to travel, so the decision itself wasn't unusual. What made the choice a little bizarre was our decision to go even though we could only be there for four nights. We live on the west side of Canada where there are no direct flights to San Jose. Our adventure involved 3 flights each way, and an overnight on a plane or in an airport.

I started out being a little embarrassed to tell people our plans because it was so unconventional. The more I thought about it, the more I realized it was an adventure of a life-time, the sort of thing you tend to do when you are much younger. This was an impulsive decision. We could have put it off until we had more time to enjoy the country, but we didn't, we decided to have an adventure now.

Only being in Costa Rica for four days had some unplanned benefits. We were aware of how short our visit was, so we lived it to the fullest and enjoyed every minute of it. I had planned to work on this book while I was there, but that didn't go according to plan. My decision to enjoy our mini break is one I don't regret in the slightest, even though it put my book project behind schedule.

Having goals is important, but remember to balance your focus on the future with living in the now.

The Principle

Theory without action is just an interesting read. If you want to make changes in your life, you must act on the theories you learn. A precept is a principle that leads to action. I'm so happy you're reading this book, but if you don't ignite yourself into action, this movement to improve the mental health of young people won't get off the ground. Find ways to act on the precepts, building them into your life so you can model happiness.

Action

1. Start today

Regardless of how nervous you feel about acting on your knowledge, there is no time like the present. You won't feel any less nervous tomorrow, so get started. Remember, the first step is often the most difficult.

2. Just do it

    Your plan doesn't need to be perfect before you act on it. For many people, waiting for the perfect plan toward a perfect goal is just a way of procrastinating, putting off the moment of getting started.

3. Increase Your Intentional Activity

    Add more happiness-boosting intentional activities to your life. The happiness equation shows this is the best way to feel a greater sense of well-being. Examples of ways to do this are:

    a. Commit random acts of kindness

        Have you ever seen someone struggling to open a door, or reach an item off the top shelf, and instinctively offered to help? How did aiding them make you feel? For most of us it is impossible to impulsively do something that benefits someone else without smiling and feeling a pleasant inner glow that lasts for longer than you might expect.

        The benefits of performing random acts of kindness have been studied and research shows that doing an unexpected good deed makes us feel more positive. These deeds need to be initiated by the person who is carrying them out; they should not be something another person has told you to do. Having ownership of the act is important if you want to boost your happiness. Examples of random acts of kindness are:

i. Buy a coffee or muffin for the next person in line at the coffee shop

ii. Let someone merge into your lane even if the traffic isn't heavy

iii. Give someone a genuine compliment

iv. Over-tip your server

v. Let someone go ahead of you when you are waiting at the checkout

vi. Hold the door open for someone

vii. Donate to a charity

viii. Thank the bus driver

ix. Smile at a stranger

b. Set, share, and celebrate your goals

Setting goals is important for many reasons that I have already talked about, but as well as setting them, you will increase your happiness if you share them, and celebrate accomplishing them.

Don't worry if you don't reach your goal. The boost of happiness comes from trying to attain them, so as long as you make every effort to do that, you will boost your good feelings.

If someone else knows your plan, you will be more invested in it. It is more difficult to give up when other people know what you are hoping to achieve.

Sharing your goals can provide you with support if you share them with the right people. Choose to tell friends, family, or colleagues who will listen and be there for you. I suggest you seek out people with growth mindsets.

Celebrations can be small. Take time to acknowledge your accomplishment, and let your support network join. Doing this will also increase your connection with your supporters.

c.   Keep a journal

Reflection is an important part of the learning experience for adults, and a journal can help you do that. By recording your journey, you can see the progress you've made when times get tough and it feels like you haven't accomplished anything at all.

This is also the perfect place to record a daily intention and gratitudes. Both are intentional activities that boost happiness.

Record what you intend your day to be like. Remember that your brain only processes a small amount of the information it receives. Draw its attention to the things you want to see evidence of. Think about your intention throughout your day, and reflect on it at the end.

Think about, and if possible record, three things that you are grateful for every day. Choose different things as much as possible, and be specific about why you are grateful for them.

Encourage children to keep a journal. Journaling can involve drawing pictures, or writing in sentences, phrases, or keywords. It is never too early to start setting intentions and being grateful. This activity will also support learning to live in the moment.

4. Surround yourself with positivity

    Remember that moods are contagious. Make sure you are catching the positive ones, and providing happy moods for others to catch.

5. Take care of yourself

    What's good for the body is good for the brain.

    a. Exercise, eat well, and get plenty of sleep

    b. Take twenty minutes every day to do something for you

    c. Spend time outside regardless of the weather; taking a walk can make all the difference to how you feel

6. Adjust and adapt

    Stay mindful about your journey. Adjust your course and remain adaptable. Don't think that changing your direction is a sign of failure. You will be learning as you travel; using that new knowledge to make adjustments is the sign of a good navigator.

Conclusion

It may seem a little odd that one of the precepts is about action, when every precept is a principle that leads you to action, but actually getting yourself started is one of the most difficult things to do. All the knowledge in the world won't make any difference to your life if you aren't willing to act on it.

My own personal brand of procrastination involves the belief that knowing more will make the action I take even better. If I hadn't learned to recognize that pattern of behavior, I would still be at my computer now gathering data. I am still reading and learning, but I am also acting on my vision, not just thinking about it.

If you want to create change, you must act. The first step is the hardest, and while the subsequent steps aren't easy, they are easier. It's simpler to stay in motion than it is to put yourself into motion.

Thinking out of your comfort zone is a much less threatening activity, because no one has to know you are doing it. Stepping out of your comfort zone is an act that may be seen by others. Choosing to act on the information you gather is essential if you want to join the world of change makers. You must decide to be visible if you are going to be heard.

Precept 8 – Be Part of Something Bigger

We make a living by what we get;
We make a life by what we give.

Winston Churchill

I have a memory of watching the Oprah Winfrey Show many years ago, back when I was in my twenties. She said that the thing that made her happiest was her work with charities. This stuck in my mind, because it was something I had never considered before. As my life progressed, I heard this same sentiment from many other people. It wasn't until I was doing research for my first book that I found studies to support her statement.

Research supports giving as a powerful way to increase happiness and attain personal growth. A study on charitable giving showed that your brain reacts to altruistic acts in the same way it does to pleasure rewards. Both give you a warm glow that is associated with happiness. Studies also provide data that suggests we are hardwired to have a selfless concern for the well-being of others.

If you want happiness for an hour, take a nap.
If you want happiness for a day, go fishing.
If you want happiness for a year, inherit a fortune.
If you want happiness for a lifetime, help somebody.

Chinese Saying

Perception plays a part in giving; if you do it because you feel guilted or shamed into it, you are unlikely to feel good about it and therefore won't experience a boost of happiness. It isn't about how *much* you give, but how *good* you feel about giving. Money isn't the only way to contribute to others; giving your time can be even more valuable than handing over a cheque. The important factor is that it comes from your heart.

Something Bigger Than You

In Precept #4: Change Your Perspective, I wrote about research carried out by Amy Wrzesniewski.

The data she collected during her study of what makes people happy at work revealed three orientations, or ways, that people view the work they do. You may view your work as a job, a career, or a calling. These three orientations are split fairly evenly between the working population.

If you see your work as a job, you are doing it for the money and other benefits it provides. Perhaps it allows you to work only during school hours, or has a salary that allows you to afford the life-style you want.

With a career orientation, you see the work you do as a stepping stone to advancement. If you want to manage your own store one day, you accept that you must work your way up the career ladder.

Those people who see the work they do as a calling believe that their job serves a bigger purpose than what it does just for them and their family. They believe they are part of a bigger picture. In Wrzesniewski's study of hospital janitors, those who saw themselves as caring professionals believed that their work was a calling. They worked for their salary, but enjoyed what they did because it was serving others.

During my teaching career, I experienced all three of these orientations at different times. When I entered my first classroom I was full of future possibilities and saw myself as having a career. I envisioned myself moving up to a department head and vice principal and then maybe to becoming a principal.

After a year or two, I realized that I loved being in the classroom and didn't want to sacrifice that by being an administrator. My orientation had changed to a calling. I saw myself making a difference in the lives of the students I taught, and helping to shape future generations.

When I became a mom, my reason for working took a different direction. My priority became my young children, and although I still enjoyed teaching, my focus was to have as much time as possible with my family. I quit my full-time job at a prep school and found a local part-time position. I hated the work as I felt I was more of a babysitter than a teacher, but I was willing to endure it because it meant I had more time at home. My main purpose in going to work was for the pay cheque and the time it gave me at home. Teaching had become a job for me.

Which orientation did I enjoy the most? Without a doubt, I was happiest when I saw myself as having a calling.

How This Increases Happiness

Studies show that people who perceive that their life has meaning and purpose experience healthy changes at the cellular level.

The need for relatedness that contributes to the Self-Determination Theory applies not only to feeling you belong among your social networks, but also in your larger community. Seeing yourself as being part of a bigger picture helps satisfy your need to feel linked to the world around you. This leads to a higher level of motivation, something many students, young people and adults are lacking.

Peter Warr lists one of the Needed Nine Features of Happiness as having a valued role. If you perceive yourself as being part of a bigger picture, something that is necessary for the well-being of others, you are likely to view yourself as having a valued role.

You may not want a lot of public recognition, but it is important to feel what you do is valuable. There is a lot of variation in what each one of us sees as a valued role. Don't assume that your definition is universal. Your feelings of worth may come from your own value system, the company you work for, or the society you live in. People in any job need to see themselves as valued if they are going to be happy.

Staying at home and looking after young children is very rewarding, but also incredibly hard work. You are on call 24/7, and yet there is no paycheque given to you at the end of each month. Surprisingly, parents who stay home are often happy because they see themselves as having a valued role. What is more important than making sure your children get a good start in their lives?

The Principle

Humans are social creatures, and although you are wired to survive, you are also wired to care about the community you live in. Seeing the things you do as being part of a bigger picture, and taking the time to improve the lives of others and positively change the world around you, is important if you want robust happiness.

Action

1. See yourself as one piece in a larger puzzle

   If you want to increase your self-motivation, see yourself as part of a larger community, or involved in a purpose bigger than just yourself. You are a thread in a tapestry. On your own you are just a thread, together you are a stunning design.

   Create volunteer opportunities for students of all ages. Find opportunities for your children to volunteer their time, or to assist you while you are volunteering.

2. See yourself as part of a team

   Encourage your family or class members to help with chores for the good of the unit, not because they must to earn their allowance or be allowed out for recess.

3. Model the role of a charity-minded person

   Be a volunteer; take time to help people in need, and give to charities and non-profit organizations that have a vision you agree with. Remember, there are more ways to give than just with money.

4. View the work you do as a calling

   View your work as a teacher or parent as a calling. You are teaching and raising the next generation of leaders and change makers.

5. Create a school or family community

Create a school community that everyone feels they are an active part of. The standards they help establish when they are one of the older students in the school will influence those coming up behind them. Design opportunities for students to help others. You don't have to be an academic superstar to effectively help children younger than yourself. Research shows that the best way for anyone to learn is to teach a skill to someone else. Take advantage of this solution which benefits everyone. Make learning a community affair.

Help children and youths develop a habit of doing things for others that do not benefit themselves in any way. As a family, class, grade, or school, support a charity. Make sure you choose something that aligns with the values of the people involved. Children helping other children can make a powerful impression. Try, if possible, to let the students or family members help select the charity. This fits with a need for autonomy and makes the decision more meaningful.

6. Explain to students why the things they are learning are part of the curriculum

    Give school skills and assignments context and a reason to be learned. If students understand the purpose of what they are learning, it is easier for them to accept it should be learned. If possible, create assignments that are meaningful for students. You may be able to let them help decide what books to read or topics to research.

7. Make choices that will benefit others, not just yourself

Help your students/children to see they are part of a much bigger community. Their actions make a difference to the environment and society. Be good to the earth and to each other.

Conclusion

It would be very difficult to live your life without giving to others, but do you consciously give without any expectation of personal gain? This is the key to charity that makes you feel happier. If you are looking for a way to take happiness-boosting action, charity work may be a great area to explore. There are many worthy organizations looking for volunteers. Start with one project or block of time, to ensure that the charity or non-profit is a good fit for you. If it isn't, try another one.

If you change the perspective you use to view your work, you may feel more committed to your job and leave each day with a greater feeling of satisfaction. Concentrate on how what you do helps other people. If you are a parent, change the perspective you use to view your parenting duties. Raising well-adjusted, robustly happy children is one of the most valuable contributions you can make to society.

Section IV –
Final Thoughts

Summary of the Precepts

#1 Enjoy the Journey

Life is a journey; happiness comes from being in control of the path you take. When children are very young, they need to be led and guided, but it is important to hand the reins to them as they mature. Start small, but ensure that they have practiced the skills and strategies they need to live a robustly happy life.

Recognizing that everyone has their own trek to take makes it easier to move away from a position of judgement. As long as the choices that other people make are not harming anyone, there is no reason for you to believe you know better. Acceptance is one of the greatest ways to create a nurturing community.

#2 Develop a Growth Mindset

Develop a growth mindset. See failure as an opportunity to learn, and don't think the stumbles you make define you as a person. Failing an exam does not mean you are a failure.

Make sure you praise effort and learning, not natural ability or intelligence. Ensure the words you say encourage yourself and others to adopt a growth mindset, rather than a fixed one. With a growth mindset, you will become a life-long learner. The intelligence you are born with is only the starting point, it's where you go from there that is important.

#3 Be Curious

You are programmed to learn through curiosity. Encourage your students and family to nurture and retain their feelings of inquisitiveness. If you wonder about something, take the time to find out the answer. Keep your eyes open for opportunities to learn more about yourself and the world around you.

Honor questions; don't laugh at or ridicule a query that seems obvious or silly to you. If your students/children feel comfortable asking anything, then they will continue to feel safe admitting they don't know something.

There are very few original questions. If one person doesn't understand something, chances are they aren't alone. I used to tell my students that their questions helped me as a teacher. It allowed me to understand the lessons I hadn't taught clearly enough, and gave me a chance to improve.

#4 Make Decisions and Take Responsibility

It takes courage to make a decision and stand by it, especially if other people disagree with you. It is easier to do with a growth mindset, where you see failure as an opportunity to learn. Model decision making skills, and make sure you openly demonstrate how you take responsibility for their results.

Decision making is a vital skill that improves with practice. Encourage students/children to make decisions and take responsibility for them. Don't provide them with a safety net, but be there to help them learn and recover from the experience if they need you.

#5 Change Your Perspective

Happiness is all about choice. Choose how you are going to

react to circumstances, and how you are going to interpret the events you observe. The glass is both half-full and half-empty, you get to choose which version you want to believe.

Take time to demonstrate how different viewpoints can be used to see the same situation. Be mindful of looking for a win-win solution or perspective when other people are involved.

#6 Connect with Others

Humans are hardwired to connect with others. It doesn't matter how introverted you think you are, you still need to have social connections. Don't underestimate the importance of this; nurture your existing relationships, and be willing to invest time to develop new ones.

Social connection is vital for happiness, and as a result schools need to ensure every student feels they are accepted and belong to the community. Take time to get to know each person you teach, and let them get to know you; this is an important piece of the school culture and close family-unit puzzles.

#7 Take Action

Change won't happen unless you choose to act. This is the most important precept if you want to make a difference in the world. How you behave is the example you are setting for the impressionable minds that are watching you. Knowing how to be happy is of no use unless you embody the precepts. Give the people around you a realistic example of what a happy life can look like.

If you find it difficult to act, then it is all the more important to take the plunge. The big difference between most dreams that become reality and those that don't is the willingness of the dreamer to take action. Reading this book won't help change the world unless you are willing to put these philosophies into practice. Don't wait until you feel perfectly prepared; that is just a form of procrastination. Be brave and start now.

#8 Be Part of Something Bigger

Look for a way of seeing yourself as part of a bigger picture. You can focus on your work or personal life, but find a way to help the larger community you live in. This can be at a local, national, or international level. Model this way of thinking and behaving for your students/children.

Give children the chance to see themselves as part of a bigger picture. How can they make a small change in the world? Set goals that have no personal payoff for you, your family or your students. Help them understand that every puddle starts with a single drop of rain.

Getting Started

I hope you feel as motivated to be part of the Modelling Happiness movement as I am. If you are, then it is important that you act. Take small steps. You can't change the world in one day. Even epic journeys start with a single stride.

Start by becoming aware of your thoughts and behaviors. Would you be proud if others copied them? What can you do to adjust?

Choose one precept and think of a single way you can move towards adopting it. Write it down. Create a strategy to make it happen. If you decide your first step is to develop a growth mindset, you might enlist the help of a friend or family member to help you realize when you slip back into a fixed mindset, then change your words, thoughts, or actions to reflect your new way of thinking.

I love to be surrounded by words and quotes that encourage me on my path. Put messages on your desk, pictures on your walls, and post-its on your mirror. It is important to remain conscious of the step you have chosen to take. When you feel you have a handle on that step, choose another one.

Share the precepts with others; this will add accountability to your journey. If your friends, family, students, and colleagues know about your intentions, they will become a network for both support and responsibility. Embody the principles. If you live and believe them, then your enthusiasm will attract others to their magic.

Advice for Schools

A teacher affects eternity;
He can never tell where his influence stops.'

Henry Adams (American Historian)

You have a tremendous amount of impact on the lives of your students. You may never know the effect you have on the children who pass through your classroom, but rest assured that many will remember you. Make sure you inspire them to believe in themselves and the differences they can make in the world. A tiny pebble can start a large ripple.

Every adult in your school, regardless of whether they are part of the teaching staff or not, needs to be modelling these eight precepts if you want to change your school culture to its very core. Support each other and allow opportunities for professional development.

That isn't to say you shouldn't change the culture in your classroom, even if the rest of the school isn't on board yet. Teaching and applying the precepts in your classroom will ensure your students have a safe place to learn. You can be the pebble that starts the ripple in your school.

Use your brilliance as a teacher to find those golden teachable moments. This will happen naturally if you believe in and model the precepts. Be open about your feelings, struggles, and learning opportunities. By sharing a little about how you cope with life, you will create a stronger bond with your students and teach them that everyone's journey has challenges.

Use the vocabulary of the precepts throughout the school. This will make communication and discussion easier for everyone. Don't forget how important understanding is. Include the science behind the precepts whenever it is appropriate. Knowledge is powerful.

Advice for Parents

Your children may not be listening to you,
but they are definitely watching you.

As children, we copy the actions of the significant adults in our lives, often without question. So many of the methods I have adopted are the ones I saw my mother exhibit. 'Monkey see, monkey do,' is far more than just an expression. When those little monkeys are looking at you, are they copying behaviors that you want them to adopt?

In T. Harv Eker's book, *Secrets of the Millionaire Mind*, he tells the story of a woman who cuts off the ends of a ham before she cooks it. When her husband asks her why, she says that was the way her mom did it. When her mother arrives for dinner, they ask her why she cut the ends off the ham. She replies by saying that's the way her mom cooked it. They phone Grandma to ask her why she prepared the ham that way, and she told them it was because her pan was too small to hold the ham, so she cut the ends off to make it fit. Without question, each generation followed the same process for cooking a ham, even though it was no longer necessary to do so.

Start by examining your own beliefs and behaviors. Do they fit with the precepts in this book? Model the person you want your children to become. Honor the fact that every family member has their own path to follow and lessons to learn. Saving them from difficult times is not helpful. Let them experience life in all its forms, and be there to help them if they stumble or fall.

Use the vocabulary from the precepts. This common language will make it easier for you to communicate. Don't think that you need to have everything figured out. You are on your own journey of discovery, and will continue to learn throughout your entire life.

Encourage schools to become part of the Modelling Happiness movement, and suggest the Parent Advisory Council/Parent Teacher Association get involved. Having a support system of other parents will make the learning process easier.

Conclusion

Be a light not a judge.
Be a model not a critic.

Stephen Covey

I set out to write a book that would encourage teachers and parents to help improve the mental wellness of the world by modelling what a happy life looks like. Don't be misled into thinking that happiness is something you can capture; it is a philosophy, a way of life, an attitude. By making a commitment to become a happiness model for today's children, youths, and young adults, you will be joining me in this mission to transform the world.

If I had known that I was the key to my own happiness, or had some understanding of emotions and the happiness skills I needed when my life nose-dived, I don't think I would have sunk quite so low. In spite of that, I believe there was a reason for me to take that journey. Mental health issues have always been present, but they are affecting the younger generations more now than ever before. If this book helps just one person, then *Modelling Happiness* will be a success.

You may believe that your students and children are happy, and maybe they are, but is it the sort of happiness that will sustain them during difficult times? Do they understand that they are in control of their own happiness? If not, they are in a very vulnerable position.

As I said in the introduction, this book is about change,

choice, and happiness. Only you can change your life into a robustly happy one; the decision is yours. Help others discover the same understanding by becoming a happiness model. Together, we can change the world, one child, one classroom, one family at a time.

Ways to Work with Reen

Reading this book is a great way to start changing the way you incorporate happiness skills in your school culture and home-life. To jumpstart this transformation, invite Reen to your professional development days. Her workshops are for everyone who works in the school, regardless of whether they have a teaching role or not. Reen will introduce the precepts, help you understand why they are so important, and give you a multitude of ways to include the 'Modelling Happiness' program in your everyday curriculum and support roles.

Combine this day of development with a PAC presentation that will help parents understand and support the philosophy of the school. Not only will their children be mentally healthier and more prepared to deal with the challenges of life, but when put into practice, each family unit will be stronger and more cohesive.

For more information about Reen Rose and the services and programs she provides:

1. Check out her website at www.ModellingHappiness.com

2. Contact her at info@ModellingHappiness.com

3. Like her Facebook page

www.Facebook.com/ModellingHappiness

Additional Support

If you are looking for support material for primary classrooms, try www.redsandkids.com. Sandy and Maria create books and activities that fit beautifully with the modelling happiness program. Many of the activities are available at no cost on their website.

Recommended Reading

Anchor, S. (2010). *The Happiness Advantage*. New York: Random House.

Diener, E., & Biswas-Diener, R. (2008). *Happiness Unlocking the Mysteries of Psychological Wealth*. Malden: Blackwell Publishing.

Diener, E., & Seligman, M. E. (2002). Very Happy People. *Psychological Science*, Vol. 13, No. 1, p 81-84.

Doidge, N. M. (2007). *The Brain That Changes Itself*. New York: Penguin Books.

Doidge, N. P. (2016). *The Brain's Way of Healing*. New Yorl: Penguin Books.

Dweck, C. S. (2008). *Mindset: The New Psychology of Success*. New York: Random House.

Frederick, S., & Loewenstein, G. (1999). Hedonic Adaptation. In D. Kahneman, *Wellbeing: The Foundations of Hedonic Psychology* (pp. 302-329). New York: Russel Sage Foundation.

Fredrickson, B. L. (2012). Positive Emotions Broaden and Build. *Advances on Experimental Social Psychology*.

Lindsay, C. (2011, 08 22). *Why People need Social Interaction*. Retrieved 2014, from sciences360.com.

Lyubomirsky, S. (2007). *The How of Happiness*. New York: Penguin Books.

Lyubomirsky, S. (2010, 08 03). *Hedonic Adaptation to Positive and Negative Experiences*. Retrieved 2014, from psychologytoday.com.

Lyubomirsky, S. (2013). *The Myths of Happiness*. New York: Penguin Books.

Maurer, R. P. (2014). *One Small Step Can Change Your Life*. Workman Publishing Company, Inc.

Medina, J. (2008). *Brain Rules*. Seattle WA: Pear Press.

Pink, D. H. (2009). *Drive*. New York: Penguin Books.

selfdeterminationtheory.org. (n.d.).

Seligman, M. (2002). *Authentic Happiness*. New York: The Free Press.

Seligman, M. (2011). *Flourish, A Visionary New Understanding of Happiness and Well-being*. New York: Atria.

Warr, P., & Clapperton, G. (2010). *The Joy of Work? Jobs, Happiness, and You*. New York: Routledge.

About the Author

Reen Rose is an experienced, informative, and engaging speaker, author, and educator, based in the beautiful Okanagan area of British Columbia. She has worked for over three decades in the world of education, teaching children and adults in Canada and England.

Her presentations and workshops are a wonderful blend of research-based expertise, storytelling, humor, and practical strategies. Reen believes in equipping individuals with the tools they need to be happy and successful. She is a Myers Briggs certified practitioner, a Microsoft Office certified trainer, and a qualified and experienced teacher.

This happy-preneur is on a mission to boost mental well-being throughout the world by making the inclusion of happiness skills part of every school's philosophy. Reen is dedicated to increasing levels of success, satisfaction, and spirit - one child, one classroom, one school at a time.

Made in the USA
Monee, IL
08 April 2021